LOVED & SENT

How Two Words Define
WHO YOU ARE AND WHY YOU MATTER

TENTH
POWER

Elgin, IL · Tyler, TX

TENTHPOWERPUBLISHING
www.tenthpowerpublishing.com

Design by Inkwell Creative
Softcover ISBN 978-1-938840-11-1
e-book ISBN 978-1-938840-12-8
10 9 8 7 6 5 4 3

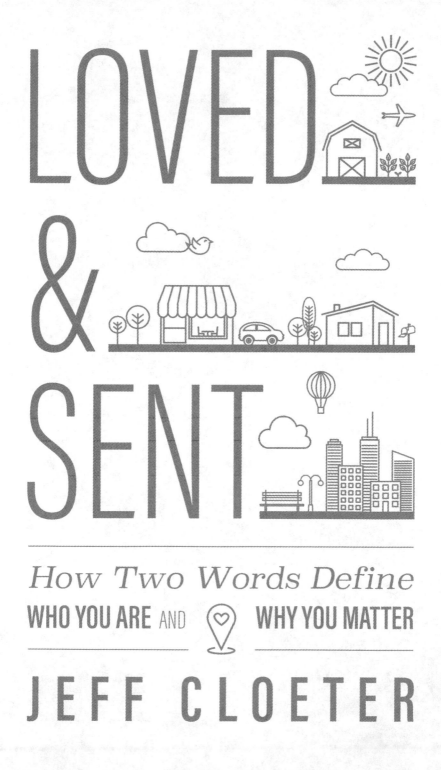

LOVED & SENT

How Two Words Define
WHO YOU ARE AND WHY YOU MATTER

JEFF CLOETER

With personal and poignant stories, Cloeter unpacks the fundamental truths of God's love for us in Christ and of his sending us into the world as his special people. This is effective catechesis through storytelling, fully informed by biblical theology, that brings God's truths about life into the very real contexts of our day-to-day living.

Dr. Andrew Bartelt
Professor of Exegetical Theology, Concordia Seminary, St. Louis, MO

When I first met Jeff Cloeter, I was 22, searching for direction, and in need of something to hold onto. When he asked me if I wanted to grab a cup of coffee, I did not hesitate to say "yes." Jeff reminded me I was loved by God and sent by him. These two words shifted the entire trajectory of my life. Through this book Jeff helps us discover who we are and why we matter. Through story and vulnerable honesty he shares the same beautiful truth he once shared with me: you are loved by God and sent by God.

Tanner Olson
Writer, Writtentospeak.com, Austin, TX

This book is profoundly personal. The stories of real people searching for real meaning and identity will instantly draw you in and keep you engaged. These personal stories, however, have a subtle way of inviting you to explore your own life as well. Cloeter makes a compelling argument for how two simple words—Loved and Sent—can be a clear witness to the Gospel of Jesus Christ.

Rev. A. Trevor Sutton
author of *Being Lutheran* and *Why Should I Trust the Bible?*

This is a great book! Identity. Purpose. Vision. You'll see yourself differently. You'll see the world differently. You'll see the church differently. Cloeter makes words sing and carefully fuses them together to stir your soul. It will move you to action. "For every Christian, there exists a point where *who God is* intersects with *who I am.*" I recommend this book!

Dr. Jock Ficken
Executive Leader, Pastoral Leadership Institute

Loved and Sent is all about the work of Jesus in your life and in the lives of the people around you. Cloeter will help you take the basics of the Christian faith and use them to tell your story in a compelling way. Since Jeff is my pastor and close friend, I can personally attest that this is just how he and his family live every day . . . loved and sent.

Rev. Ben Haupt
Professor of Practical Theology, Concordia Seminary, St. Louis, MO

Jeff Cloeter is a leader who knows a lot about standing on the threshold. He stands on a generational threshold as a young Gen-X and old Millennial. He leads a multi-faceted congregation engaging the thresholds of a community. Jeff raises a family in an urban location that is moving through the doorway of blighted to thriving. This context provides insight for helping people loved by God become sent by Him. Jeff has anchored us to the most trustworthy foundation for thriving in thresholds. We are loved because Jesus has come. We are sent with purpose and promise for the days ahead.

Rev. Dr. Scott Seidler
Senior Pastor, Concordia Lutheran Church, Kirkwood, MO

Loved and Sent is an engaging story with a very rich, yet simple to understand message. Jeff Cloeter addresses two of life's most pressing questions: *Who am I? Why am I?* He provides meaningful insight both to people wrestling with what it means to be a Christian, as well as to people who are active in their Christian faith.

Andrew Neumann, Ph.D.
CEO of Open Sky Education, Milwaukee, WI

Who are you? What are you made for? They seem like simple questions, but their answers are quickly convoluted and confusing. What a blessing Jeff shares in reminding us that at our core we are "Loved and Sent" by God in Christ Jesus. Jeff argues for the importance of every follower of Jesus to speak his or her faith clearly, concisely, consistently, and in a compelling manner. In this book he helps us by doing so himself. What a great guide to employ as we make disciples of Jesus who make more disciples!

Aaron Putnam
City Director, LINC Bay Area, CA

For Mom and Dad.
For my Bride, Bobbi.
For Bella, Joshua, Emily, and Jacob.

In memory of Don Hannah.

CONTENTS

INTRODUCTION 11
IDENTITY AND PURPOSE 17
LOVED AND SENT 21

ONE WHO IS GOD? 31
FATHER 35
SON 43
HOLY SPIRIT 53

TWO WHO AM I? 63
GRACE 69
WORD 79
COMMUNITY 91

THREE WHAT IS GOD'S PURPOSE? 105
CREATION 111
REDEMPTION 115
SANCTIFICATION 119

FOUR WHAT IS MY PURPOSE? 125
LOVE 131
CALLING 143
GO 157

CONCLUSION 173

INTRODUCTION

The young woman sitting across from him in the café was prepared to unleash an assault. Ava began by identifying herself. "I am a lesbian atheist." As she spoke the words, her eyes examined the person across the table for a reaction. *What will the Christian man say?*

Ava and Jacob were acquaintances. They shared overlapping social spheres but didn't know each other well. What Jacob did know was that Ava was prickly. He was confused when she asked to have coffee with him. *Is this a date?* he wondered. After her declaration, he was pretty sure it wasn't.

"I'm a lesbian atheist." Ava was intentionally provocative. She knew very few Christians. The handful of religious people she did know were annoying, if not repulsive. Jacob was different, at least what she knew of him. He seemed intelligent and generous. Whenever she talked with him, he was sincerely interested in her. And she heard that he actually *believed* in Jesus. It was hard for her to reconcile this dichotomy: an intelligent and generous Christian, and one with genuine conviction.

She paused for Jacob to react, but he felt it best not to counter. "Tell me your story," he said, hoping to push past an awkward silence. "We've only hung out a couple times. Mark's house, I think." He smiled nervously.

Ava accepted his invitation and embarked on a 20-minute overview of her life. Under the prickly exterior were the tragic death of a sister and the sting of her father's affair when she was a child. She alluded to a period of substance abuse. He noticed scars on her wrists. And when she wasn't looking at him, she defaulted to a nervous glance behind her. It was as if she expected someone to attack.

When she concluded, Jacob responded, "I had no idea, Ava." He wasn't sure what to say. This was not the conversation he expected. "Is there anything I can do?"

"Well, what *can* you do?" she asked while watching a toddler spill a glass of orange juice on the other side of the diner. "It's life. It sucks."

"I'll pray for you." As Jacob completed the sentence, he realized his offer to pray wouldn't mean much to an atheist.

"You Christians," Ava replied. "You just push your religion anywhere you can." Her volume increased. "You want to legislate your morality. You judge people and preach. But you don't really care . . ." She trailed off, like she wanted to say more, but restrained herself.

As Ava was speaking, she realized that Jacob did seem to care. She stared at him through the silence, curious to hear his response. She examined him with a look that spoke, *Who is the straight, white, Christian man who's willing to listen to a lesbian atheist?*

Ava nodded toward Jacob, indicating that it was his turn to speak. Bluntly, she stated, "So you asked about my story. Now it's your turn. I mean, who are you?" He took a deep breath in the little diner. *What should I say?*

As Christians, we often stutter when questioned. *Who are you? What do you believe? Why does it matter to you?* If someone quizzed you about your core convictions, could you give a coherent answer? Could you do it concisely, in one or two sentences?

Every Christian ought to have a clear and compelling statement about who they are. But too often we fumble. We get a unique chance to share our heart and we say too much or nothing at all.

In an increasingly non-Christian American society, Christians hold to a faith that is more and more a distant memory. True Christianity is muddled by varying opinions about Jesus. Or the message is overwhelmed by a thousand competing narratives.

Non-Christians often have misperceptions about Christianity. Or they confuse Christian culture for the Christian faith. **New Christians** are overwhelmed and intimidated. **Mature Christians** are unable to convey their faith in an understandable way.

In this era, it is of critical importance for every follower of Jesus to speak of his or her faith clearly, concisely, consistently, and in a compelling manner.

CLEAR

Can you clearly communicate the heart of the Christian message? The modern world is inundated with the chaotic noise of a million voices shouting for attention. Christians easily devolve into religious obscurity. Can you speak clearly enough that the person listening to you can repeat your message in one sentence?

CONCISE

Our interactions with people are often brief. If you speak your deepest convictions, you probably have a short window in which to do it. Can you share the heart of your faith in 60 seconds? Modern media has trained us to pay attention in short intervals. This is not to undermine the necessity of longer explanation, but if we can't summarize our message in one minute, we'd be challenged to do it in 60 minutes.

CONSISTENT

If you asked 10 Christians what the Gospel is, you may well get 10 different responses. Consistent doesn't mean that it's rigidly scripted. The Bible uses a variety of language and metaphors to express the Gospel, yet the core of the message is fundamentally consistent.

COMPELLING

In a world of competing narratives, what makes the Christian story uniquely compelling? What is so gripping about Jesus? Why would we ever devote our entire lives to a first-century carpenter executed as a criminal? Christians must know the uniquely compelling components of the Christian narrative. They must lift up the features that differentiate this story from all others. What makes Jesus unique?

In the chaos and confusion of modern society, we long for honest truth that cuts through all the noise and distraction. *What really matters? What's most important? What would I die for?*

I am a straight, white, middle-class male. But in many ways, I have felt the same tension as Ava, a self-described lesbian atheist. No matter our self-definition, we are both human beings. We share common experiences of sorrow and joy, failure and freedom. Our lives are distinctly different and yet strangely familiar.

Ava asked Jacob, "Who are you?" Before Jacob can answer that question for Ava, he must answer it for himself. She doesn't need a religiously cluttered response. The millions of "Avas" in our society aren't interested in sterile statements cut and pasted out of a book. They want a real answer from a real person.

Like Jacob, I take a deep breath before answering, "Who are you?" In the following pages I share my own quest to answer this basic question. I begin with just two words: **Loved. Sent.** They summarize who I am and what my purpose is. In many respects, they characterize the whole Christian message. Let me tell you how I came to these words and why they are so powerful.

Reflect

> Think about your faith. Do you find it difficult to be clear, concise, consistent, and compelling in speaking what you believe? Which of the four is most challenging?

> Ava may be a provocative personality, but those who question Christianity take many forms. You may have close friends or family members who are distant from the Christian faith. When you think of the Avas in your life, what are their biggest concerns?

> If you are an Ava who happens to be reading this, do you know any Christians who, like Jacob, are "intelligent and generous"? What is your general experience with people who believe in Jesus?

IDENTITY AND PURPOSE

Even today, my stomach turns at the scent of a newly waxed hardwood gym floor. Mixed with the stale smell of old sweat, it reminds me of the most horrifying day of my adolescence. Yet this haunting junior high memory would fuel a larger quest.

I was six feet tall in eighth grade and still growing. My body was long, angular, and awkward. At the top of my head was a helmet of full-bodied hair. Add glasses and acne, and I was a spectacular mess.

My home was the rugged woods and rocky bluffs of Michigan's Upper Peninsula. Bessemer is a rural mining and logging town near Lake Superior. In this small town, I had an eighth-grade class of only 22 students.

The junior high dance played out predictably—boys on one side and girls on the other in the dim light of the school's gymnasium. A few rebels met in the middle, bouncing to dance jams that echoed off the gym walls.

When the music slowed, larger numbers of students migrated to uncomfortable embraces and rotational shuffling. During the first slow dance, a message was relayed to me from Peter Jenkins that Jen Anderson wanted to dance with me. Jen was tall, athletic, and popular.

This piece of information was just enough to push me beyond my comfort zone. The next song was "Every Rose Has Its Thorn" by Eighties hair band Poison. The song title was an omen of disaster.

I navigated the dance floor toward female territory. I approached Jen. Her hair was perfect. Her smile was soft and warm. I attempted to speak over the blaring music: "Do . . . do you want to dance?" "What?!" she shouted. I increased my volume and squeaked, "Do you want to dance?!" "Uh . . . okay."

I remember that we stopped at the free-throw line of the basketball court. I held her at a distance. We both stared over the other's shoulder, avoiding eyes. I wanted to say something, but my mind was ticking like a metronome, trying to keep the rhythm. We shuffled in a circle, rotating like a rotisserie chicken, and I soon felt roasted.

It wasn't until I returned to the boys' side that I was informed of Peter Jenkins' devious plan. Jen had not requested a dance with me, but was awaiting another candidate. Peter was bent over in laughter. The music kept going, but the mood felt like silence. I stood on the sideline, alone.

Adolescent embarrassment is a rite of passage. We all recount the red-faced shame of a horrendous experience. It is these moments that transfer us from innocent play to the deep, fundamental questions of adulthood. *Does anyone like me? Am I worth anything? Where do I belong? Who will take me?* From this teen angst, I began to ask two questions that would carry on through my life's story.

Who am I? What is my purpose? Though we rarely vocalize these questions, every human being is on a quest to answer them. From the kindergartner to the nursing home resident, from the liberal activist to the religious zealot. Everyone is seeking these basic human needs: **identity and purpose.**

Typically we aren't conscious of these foundational questions, but they influence our most important decisions in life. Our schooling and work, our dreams and aspirations—they all attempt to validate who we are and why we matter.

In a global society, we are increasingly confronted by a crisis of identity and meaning. Even with mountains of knowledge at our fingertips, many believe that there is no transcendent meaning in the world. Meaning is reduced to an individual's own experience and interpretation. *But what really counts? What transcends? What matters above all else?*

As a shy, skinny teenager, I began an earnest search for identity and meaning. I tried to be Michael Jordan, but the NBA never called. I worked hard for a 4.0, but being a nerd isn't as cool as being a jock. My quest turned toward God. If he created me, he must have some say in who I am and what my purpose is.

At 14 years old, I took my first serious look at the Bible. We get to know a person by hearing his or her story. We know who someone is by what they've done and the experiences they've been through. The Bible is the record of God's story. It is the history of his activity. So I began to read the Bible asking the questions I wondered of myself. *Who is God? What is his purpose?*

I wasn't simply gleaning information *about* God. I wanted to *know* God. The Sunday school answers were no longer sufficient. Raw reality makes you question God's goodness. The God of the church sanctuary is fine, but what about the dance in the school gymnasium?

A disclaimer: I am a pastor's kid. Of course I would turn to the Bible, right? But it wasn't that simple. As an emerging adult, I was driven to push, question, and stretch the boundaries. Sophomore biology triggered a year of atheism. Hollywood movie stars opened my eyes to Eastern spiritualism. Locker room chatter revealed hedonism, a life lived for mere pleasure.

Still, I kept returning to the compelling claims of the Biblical record. I wasn't searching for "religion," self-help, or quick answers to complicated questions. I sincerely wanted to know what God might see in me when all I saw was a forgettable teenager from a small town. This quest would eventually lead me to two words.

Reflect

> What's the most embarrassing moment in your life? If you're in a group, consider sharing it.

> Why are identity and purpose so important? What are some common ways that people search for personal identity or purpose?

> We live in an age of unparalleled access to information. Does this make it easier or harder to answer questions of identity and purpose? Why do you think so?

LOVED AND SENT

The images on the TV screen felt like a knee to my gut. Mobs of young black men filled the streets. A reporter on the corner dashed to cover at the pop of gunshots. Then the camera shifted to a cop car ablaze. Hooded figures darted into the shadows. An aerial shot revealed a small business engulfed in flames just miles from my home on the south side of St. Louis.

On August 9, 2014, 18-year-old Michael Brown was shot by a white police officer, Darren Wilson, in Ferguson, Missouri. Brown was unarmed. There were witnesses who claimed Wilson shot him while his hands were up. It ignited a firestorm. Race, history, politics, and socioeconomics were the kindling. Michael Brown's death was the spark. "Hands up! Don't shoot!" was the rally cry. We called the event by the name of the community set ablaze—Ferguson. But it was about our whole city. St. Louis was on fire. And all of America was watching.

Now it was November. The grand jury determined that Officer Wilson would not be indicted for Brown's death. This sparked more riots. Helicopters zoomed over our house. My kids were tucked in bed. School was canceled the next day. As I watched TV, I saw the image of a building near my house. Graffiti sprayed on the brick wall threatened, "If we burn, you burn. F the police!"

Where's Brandon? I had texted him, but no response. The young black men on the television looked like Brandon. Same skin color, age, and clothes. A 22-year-old black male, Brandon would have blended into the crowd in Ferguson. I prayed that he wasn't in the streets.

Brandon has called me "brother" since he was nine years old. My wife, Bobbi, and I were 22-year-old newlyweds. We met Brandon and his two siblings through a North St. Louis church. We quickly connected. It began with tutoring and trips to the zoo, but over the years we became family. Before Bobbi and I had children, these kids gave us a taste of parental responsibility.

Brandon and I are an odd pairing. I grew up rural. Brandon never knew life outside the city limits. I grew up in the Northwoods of Michigan. Brandon grew up on the notorious North Side of St. Louis. My family was stable. His dad was in jail. My skin is white. His is black.

The first time we took Brandon to our modest apartment, he opened the pantry door and froze. I worried that something was wrong. The shelves were stocked with cans of corn and boxes of mac and cheese. He finally spoke. "Oh my God, you got food!"

So we ate food. Lots of it. That day, his nine-year-old stomach devoured mac and cheese, carrots, biscuits, frozen pizza, and a bowl of ice cream. He was filled with joy and wonder as he explored our little apartment. He asked about everything.

"What's this?"

"A picture of my family."

"That your momma and daddy?"

"Yeah. And my brother and sister."

"You only got two?"

"Yeah."

"What's this?"

"Oh, that's the deer I shot in high school."

Brandon froze. He took a step back from me. "Oh my God, you shot a gun?" "Yeah." "You killed a deer?!" "Yeah." It took me 10 minutes to assure him that hunting was legal and safe, and no humans were injured in the harvesting of the deer.

I was just as curious about Brandon's life, a world so different from my own. My quest for identity and meaning took on a new perspective when I entered Brandon's experience. For me, there was always opportunity. I had choices. I had freedom to make something of myself. But I had never encountered someone whose destiny was, in many respects, all but predetermined.

What chance did a nine-year-old black kid from the north side have? Cycles of poverty, crime, and absent fathers inflicted a generational curse. *Can't he just get out?* I once thought. But it wasn't that easy. Economics, race, and twisted social structures all collide to trap a child in a system nearly impossible to escape.

By November 2014, Brandon had outlived many of his peers. The nine-year-old boy was a 22-year-old man. I texted, "Where you at?" Finally a response came. "I'm OK. At home." I sighed. Maybe I could sleep tonight.

• • •

Ava interrogated Jacob: "Who are you?" She wasn't only interested in his answer. She was really inquiring about her own identity. We often come to answer this question for ourselves when we ask it of other people.

Asking this question through the eyes of Brandon helped me arrive at an answer. Identity and meaning are transcendent human needs. They cross boundaries of race and socioeconomic background. It's not just a white kid's problem. I had to walk next to a black kid from an urban context to fully understand the universal ache for these basic human needs.

In a search for **identity,** we long to be loved. To belong. To be accepted. We fear love's opposite: abandonment. To be placed on the shelf and forgotten seems worse than the fire of hell.

In a search for **purpose,** we long to matter to someone else. To be needed. To be respected. To be valued. To be worth something to those around us. We are terrorized by the prospect of uselessness. We fear the possibility that we might be disposable, unneeded, and tossed in the trash.

It sounds like the beginning of a bad joke. "A lesbian atheist, a black kid, and a pastor walk into a room . . ." Whether Ava, Brandon, or Jeff, we are all haunted by the possibility of our unimportance. We all yearn to fill the spaces left by questions of identity and purpose.

I believe God sent me to Brandon. And that Brandon was sent to me. This unlikely duo formed a bond of brotherly love. In this friendship we have come to know the God who *loves* and *sends.*

LOVED

What does "love" mean? I'm frustrated by the word. First of all, it is a cliché so overused in our culture that it's empty of meaning. Love can be a fuzzy feeling or emotion. It can mean a romantic sentiment like passing notes to a high school crush. Or it can mean sex. You can use the word love to describe how you feel about bacon or how you feel about your mother. So what does it really mean?

My second frustration with the word "love" is that the people who define it in our culture are the same ones who can't make love work. Pop stars and movie stars write our love songs and romantic comedies. But when is the last time you heard of a 50-year marriage in Hollywood?

We live with a perverted and denigrated use of the word "love." Love is treated as a commodity: something that is sought and then discarded. We are riding an agonizing carousel, spinning in an endless pursuit of love but never reaching it. We attempt to "get love" by being pretty, popular, or productive. But in the end, we're left empty.

The kind of love we're most familiar with is based on a certain mutuality. Love only exists when it is returned. It only grows when it is reciprocated. But what happens when it is no longer mutual? Or when it is one-sided? It's often said, "We fell out of love." There is an assumption that people eventually outgrow one love and move on to another.

There are a handful of words for love in ancient Greek, the language in which the Bible's New Testament was written. A primary word for "love" in reference to God is *agape*. *Agape* isn't "fluffy, puppy love." It's not just a feeling or an emotion. It's not based on any conditions. ("Love me, then I'll love you back.")

The Bible uses love as a verb. It is an action. More specifically, **it is the selfless act of giving yourself up for someone else.** A key example of this kind of love comes from the Apostle John: "In this is love, not that we have loved God but that he loved us and sent his Son to be the atoning sacrifice for our sins" (I John 4:10). God's love is not mere sentiment. His love compels him to deploy his own Son on a perilous mission.

Love is ultimately proven in action. You only understand the power of the word after you've seen it done in real life. Love is sacrificial. It is costly. It takes risks. It gives without conditions. It acts without the expectation of a return. It is tenacious and patient (I Cor. 13).

The primary Hebrew word for love in the Bible's Old Testament gets at a similar point. *"Hesed"* means "steadfast love." It is a "stick-with-it" kind of love. It is "day in and day out." Both Biblical words for love are reflected in the traditional wedding vows: "for better, for worse, for richer, for poorer, in sickness and in health, to love and to cherish, until death parts us, and I pledge you my faithfulness."

Love is proven when the dreamy romance is past. It emerges more in "sickness" than "in health" and more in "poorer" than in "richer." Love actively chooses to be selfless. It gives even when you're annoyed or angry. It persists long after the honeymoon. In fact, genuine love grows in unpleasant challenges. It can only be proven when tested.

This kind of love is counterintuitive. In some ways, it is madness. It confronts a "survival-of-the-fittest" worldview because it is more concerned with the survival of others than its own self-preservation. Such love even pushes the boundaries of justice because of its willingness to endure injustice for others. It asks for no return. It is recklessly generous.

For a Christian, the cross is love's ultimate symbol. We claim that the most explicit picture of love is a Roman execution device. Wood and blood, nail and spear. It is the brutal and horrific violation of justice, willingly endured by one man for the sake of a people rightfully labeled his "enemies." Yet he treated them as friends. This is love in its ultimate and purest form.

Such love is too threatening to the old order of mutuality. Thus, Jesus' unconditional expenditure of love was an offense to those who would keep score. Strangely, love got Jesus killed. At the same time, his death is proof of that very love.

Fear is often described as love's opposite. Fear breeds self-doubt, insecurity, and desperation. By contrast, self-giving love imparts worth upon the one who is loved. Even if you have no self-evident worth, the love of another bestows inherent value. Even if you were incapacitated, the love of another gives you an identity. Love's pure form is revealed precisely when you can do nothing to earn it.

"Loved" is the passive form of the word. It means that someone else is the primary subject, the one "doing" love. "Loved" means that we don't attain favor or affection. Instead it has been bestowed. We have been *given* worth and value. We are *beloved.* God has "done love" in Jesus Christ. By comparison, every other definition of love seems like cotton candy: empty sugar with no substance.

SENT

Love is incapable of sitting still. Love is not love unless it acts, moves, and gives. God puts his heart on display by the dynamic movement of *sending.* "Sent" is an active expression of love. In the Bible, whenever there is trouble, God has a way of sending help.

The word "mission" comes from the Latin word *missio,* meaning, "to send." We get to the heart of God's mission when we see him send. God sent deliverers (Ex. 4:28). God sent warriors (Judges). God sent prophets (Is. 6:8). God sent apostles (Matt. 10:5). But the pinnacle of all God's sending was a divine Rescuer. A Savior. His very Son. Again, I John 4:10: "In this is love, not that we have loved God but that he loved us and sent his Son to be the atoning sacrifice for our sins." This sending was an act of love, and love was proven in giving up a most valuable possession.

In sending Jesus, God shows love in its purest form. Men buy flowers and diamonds to show love. God sent his prized and beloved Son. Sending is the hazardous work that love is willing to undertake. Sending is risky. For Jesus, love is worth the sending and the suffering, so that you might know that you are loved by God.

God is a sending God. God the Father sent Jesus. In turn, Jesus sent his disciples. He prayed, "As you have sent **me** into the world, so I have sent **them** into the world" (John 17:18). Remarkably, the pattern of divine sending extends to us. *We* are sent. The Christian is under divine orders, deployed by Jesus with purpose.

As we'll see, the dominant theme of the Christian Scriptures is that God continues to love people even though they make themselves unlovable. This fact informs who we are. First, we are loved, forgiven, and affirmed as God's children. Then, from our *being* emerges *doing.* Jesus commands us to "go," and we are sent out in ways we never thought possible.

Out of love, God sent Jesus on a divine rescue mission. Out of that same love, Jesus sends *you.* It's such a simple statement, but *loved* and *sent* are like the tip of an iceberg. Over time, I discovered a mountain of meaning under the surface of these nine letters. They speak a substantial truth. Let me show you what loved and sent reveal about God and about you.

Reflect

> What are different ways the word "love" is used in our culture? What do you think is the most common definition?
> How is the Biblical use of the word "love" different than our common uses? For examples in the Bible, see Deut. 23:5; Jer. 31:1–3; John 3:16, 15:13; Gal. 2:20; I Cor. 13.
> How is being sent an outcome of love? For an example, see Gal. 4:1–7.
> Think of a time that your love for someone compelled you to act.

ONE

WHO IS GOD?

At one point in the conversation, Ava told Jacob, "Your belief in God is just *irrelevant*." It was one way she rationalized her atheism. "Does it matter that God exists? Or that Jesus lived? If there is a God, it's not relevant to me. All that matters is what I make of my own life."

For some, like Ava, identity is self-assigned. You determine your own self-made personhood apart from the confines of any deity or cultural norm. Similarly, many take this liberty with God. His identity seems to be in the hands of every individual. You are free to fashion a deity in your own likeness. You attempt to conform God to your own preferences.

Even those who believe in the God of the Bible wonder what kind of God they've committed to. It's one thing to talk about a broad belief system. Daily life is another. The demands of work or school. The strains of family life and friendship. The challenges of sickness and poverty. We are often confounded by God's seemingly distant nature. We wonder if he is a real and personal presence. Or maybe he's a distant being, like an uncle you occasionally call for help.

"Who is God?" Amid the marketplace of deities, the Christian faith proclaims an extraordinarily personal God. For centuries, the word "Trinity" has been used to describe *who God is.* The Bible reveals one God in three distinct persons—the Father, Son, and Holy Spirit. "Persons" is a term used to ascribe identity. In the very nature of his being, God reveals himself as **personal.**

In this vein, the Bible consistently uses personal language. The Scriptures regularly employ relational expressions like trust, longing, covenant, and the bond of parent and child. There is a consistency of the personal pronouns—God relating to "my people," and people relying on "our God."

Within these personal descriptions, we discover a God of steadfast love who continually chases a wandering people. For reasons beyond comprehension, he still chooses to love them in their lost state and send aid at great risk to himself. Here is where we discover who God is.

FATHER

I was a 21-year-old kid attempting to marry the farmer's daughter. He should have shot me. I had met Bobbi just eight months earlier. Now I was sitting across the table from Bob in a diner, asking to marry his little girl and then take her to Africa on a six-month volunteer mission. Yeah, this was a tough sell.

Bob is a barrel-chested central Wisconsin dairy farmer. He's done more work in a day than most men have in a lifetime. He once wrestled a 1,200-pound Holstein out of a manure pit. I've seen him pull a newborn calf from inside its mother using his bare hand.

A coyote was prowling his acreage one day, threatening the young cattle. While driving the edge of a cornfield he spotted the beast 200 yards away. He calmly exited the truck and walked to the back. He lowered the gate and reached for a firearm, loaded it, and then stared down the furry assassin.

The coyote fled in fear. In one fluid motion, Bob lifted the barrel and fired. With a single shot, the fleeing predator tumbled in a heap of defeat. Yes, Bob is a man's man. He conquers ravenous beasts while producing milk and cheese for the nation. And I dared to marry his daughter? Bobbi was worth it. This farmer raised an exceptional daughter, and I wanted to make her my wife.

In that little diner, I looked into his eyes as he glared at me across the table. We talked about finishing college. We discussed the future and the importance of family. But in the course of the conversation, I never directly asked for his blessing.

In a moment of nervous silence, I abruptly ended our time. "Well . . . uh . . . I'll get the bill. Talk to you later." We left the restaurant awkwardly. In my mind I kept thinking, *IDIOT!* I'd fumbled the whole thing.

I returned to Bobbi's apartment where she and her four roommates were eagerly awaiting news. "It went okay," I lied. To escape the gossipy chatter of her friends, I crashed on the couch, utterly dejected. Then there was a knock at the door. "Bobbi, your dad wants to talk to Jeff."

As I approached the door, I wondered, "Does he have a shotgun? Or maybe just a buck knife for a slower, more painful death. Or he could use his bare hands. Less blood."

Bob was alone in the corridor. The apartment door shut behind me, and I knew there were five ears pressed against it. "I want to say something to you, Jeff," he said. He extended his right hand. Forged by decades of milking cows, each finger was as thick as a sausage. Together, they formed a hand akin to a catcher's mitt. I reached out my hand. It disappeared in his.

"Bobbi is very special to me," he said. "And I want you to know that I give you my blessing to marry her. Take good care of my girl."

With the high-pitched crack of an adolescent, I replied, "Yes, sir."

Bob is a strong man, but also a tender father. He lives with the faith required of those whose livelihood depends on the weather. He speaks with the wisdom derived from generations of ancestors who have worked the land. He has deep compassion for his family and his community.

From that moment on, I was "in." Today I don't refer to him as Bob, but Dad. He took me in as his own son. I was accepted. I belong. No longer do we shake hands. Now we hug.

Every human on the planet has a father and a mother. Some parents are extraordinary. Some, like Ava, have experienced hurt and neglect from their parents. Regardless of our own parental experience, we are all affected by these relationships.

The term "God" is generally used to reference the first person of the Trinity, **the Father.** The name "Father" reveals the nature of God. As Father, God loves and cares for his people as "children." If the experience with our own fathers has been negative, this Father proves entirely different.

Even if you have an incredible dad, this one is better. He is Father in the best and fullest sense of the term. The central prayer that Jesus taught his disciples begins with a childlike address: "Father . . ." Jesus prays, expecting to be heard, answered, and cared for by his "Father in heaven." For all who have experienced failure with a dad, God redefines our experience by being Father in ways we've never seen before.

• • •

I believe in God, the Father Almighty, Maker of heaven and earth.
—The Apostles' Creed

CREATOR

This particular Father is "Almighty, Maker of heaven and earth." This means he is Creator, not creature or creation. He is the all-powerful and creative source of every being and all matter. Although the earth suffers from corruption, we believe that God still sustains and provides for it. Without this persistent activity, all creation would devolve into chaos.

Genesis records that after each day of creation, God declared what he made to be "good." It is a repetition that continues until the prized pinnacle of his creation, human beings. For them, he said, "very good" (Gen. 1:31).

Created "in the image of God" (Gen. 1:26–27; 9:6), humans are distinct from all other creatures. Unlike animals, our relationship with God is defined by love and trust, not just food and survival. We are complex beings, possessing a body, mind, and soul. We are the only creatures into whom God breathed "the breath of life" (Gen. 2:7). We alone have been given important responsibilities in and over creation.

The way in which God ordered the world provides a **blueprint** for how things are intended to function. The first two chapters of Genesis give us a glimpse of life as it was supposed to be. We view our humanity through this lens—the God-ordained way in which we were "built."

We return to his created order for guidance in any ethical, moral, or social dilemma. We hold ourselves to the high standard of the Creator's intention. We ask, "What has God meant for us from the beginning?"

DESIGNER

As Creator, God designed what it means to be human. As the grand Designer, God ordains parameters for our relationships, both with him and with others. They are summarized in the Ten Commandments.

There is a misperception that the Ten Commandments are the oppressive rules to "get in" with God. The Commandments are often treated like a scorecard. "If I just follow the rules . . ." But a closer look reveals that the commands are designed to define and defend what God created to be good.

The context of the Commandments is *not* like an orphan on the outside, nose pressed against the window, hoping to get in a house. Instead, the Commandments are like when an orphan has been adopted, given a room, clothes, and a place at the table. And then the parents say, "Now that you're in the family, here's how we live in this house."

The Father gives the Commandments to those already a part of his family, not as a way to get in. We get this sense in the preface to the Commandments, "I am the LORD your God who brought you out of Egypt, out of the house of slavery" (Ex. 20:2). Before he states the house rules, he reminds them of how he rescued them from the old house, a "house of slavery." He is not a slave master, but a tender and personal God: "your God."

Although the Commandments are stated in the negative—"you will not"—the opposite is implied—"you will." "You shall not kill" also means "you shall" help, defend, and provide for those God has placed around you. In this way, the Commandments reveal **all that we are to be.**

Unfortunately, we fall short of this design. Therefore, we also see in the Commandments **all that we are not.** Thus the Commandments both **empower** and **crush.** They empower us to be all that God intends for us. And they crush us with the knowledge that we live far from his intention. For this reason, we need his rescue.

The Commandments cover the basics of human existence. First and foremost, they define one's relationship with God (1–3). Then they define our relationship with others: family (4th), physical (5th), sexual (6th), material (7th), relational (8th), and the 9th and 10th are about coveting. In other words, even our intentions are under God's command and care.

1st: You will have no other gods before me.

2nd: You will not take the name of the Lord your God in vain.

3rd: Remember the Sabbath day to keep it holy.

4th: Honor your father and mother.

5th: You will not kill.

6th: You will not commit adultery.

7th: You will not steal.

8th: You will not bear false witness against your neighbor.

9th: You will not covet your neighbor's house.

10th: You will not covet your neighbor's wife, or his servants, his ox or donkey, or anything that is your neighbor's.

FATHER

A father desires more than obedience from his children. He lives to have a relationship of love and trust with them. Likewise, God the Father desires us to trust him in all times, not only when he is tender, but also when he is firm. The First Commandment is first because it is the Father's plea for this foundational trust. "You will have no other gods before me."

The sixteenth-century reformer Martin Luther wrote that the First Commandment is like God saying, "See to it that you let me alone be your God, and never seek another. Whatever good things you lack, look to me for it and seek it from me. And whenever you suffer misfortune and distress, come and cling to me."

The Old and New Testaments of the Bible are unified by their adamant monotheism. In other words, God's story insists that there is only **one, true God.** He alone created us, and he longs for us to trust him alone as God. In our modern era, the idea of only one God is judged to be exclusive and narrow-minded. But the Biblical record is unapologetic in its declaration of one, definitive God. Jesus affirmed a singular "way" and "truth" (John 14:6).

The Bible clearly conveys a **personal God,** possessing both inclusive and exclusive attributes. Parents desire their children to know them personally and to call them by name. As Father, God invites all humanity to relate to him as children. In this way, God demonstrates his inclusivity. He longs for all to have a saving relationship with him (Acts 17:27; I Tim. 2:4).

At the same time, a relationship with this personal God naturally includes particularity and exclusivity. In a world of competing powers, both spiritual and material, the Bible presents a singular authority. There is one who has no rivals, and no one to match his power, knowledge, or mercy (Is. 42:8; John 14:6; 20:21).

A mantra that originates in the Old Testament is, "The LORD our God, the LORD is one" (Deut. 6:4). "The Lord" is a reference to God's personal name, "Yahweh." He revealed this name to Moses out of a burning bush (Ex. 3:14). It tells us that he is distinct in his identity and uncompromising in his desire to be known personally and exclusively. He refuses to be mistaken for another god or to be assigned characteristics that are not his own.

"Trust me." Ultimately, we hear this appeal from God throughout the Bible (Ps. 4:5; Prov. 3:5). He invites us to love and obey him. His appeal is inclusive of all people. At the same time, it is a call to an exclusive relationship with one Father who is God over all. In each of us, there is a sense of longing for this relationship. We seek to fill this longing in a variety of ways. But, as St. Augustine wrote in the fourth century, "O God, our hearts are restless until they find rest in you."

• • •

After Bobbi and I were engaged, her family gave me a Christmas present. It was a farm jacket. Everyone in the family had this tan Carhartt, standard working man's apparel. It had my name embroidered on the left breast pocket under the name of the farm: GRANITE VIEW FARM. JEFF.

"I'm in," I thought.

All the presents were opened and Bob stood up. He said to me, "You're part of our family now." "Thank you," I responded. "But," he continued, "if you mess this up, we'll take the jacket back and grind your name off with a belt sander." He smiled. I wasn't sure if I should laugh or run.

In the end, I know what kind of father Bob is, just as I've come to know a greater Father. I still have my farm jacket. The name is still on it. In the same way, the Father in heaven has given me an identity based on his love. I wear that identity proudly. "I'm in."

Reflect

> Recognizing a variety of circumstances, describe your relationship with your father or a father figure. How does your experience relate, or not relate, to God the Father?

> The Bible clearly reveals God as "him." How might this be perceived in our modern age of gender equality? What are ways to uphold the integrity of the Bible and be sensitive to where people are today?

> The Ten Commandments are sometimes perceived as the heavy-handed rules of a tyrant. How are they positive statements about life? How are they reflective of a relationship with God?

> The First Commandment is offensive in a pluralistic society that espouses tolerance of many gods, points of view, or lifestyles. How does one hold to the personal and exclusive nature of God and still relate to such a culture?

SON

Brandon hurled a brick through the window of the abandoned house. It shattered an opening big enough to enter the old burned-out building. He had an accomplice, and together the two young boys crawled in.

The brick dwelling once housed German immigrants on St. Louis's north side. They fled generations ago. Today, the neighborhood residents are black. Many of their ancestors were slaves. Brandon was free, but statistics would say he had little more chance than a slave to break free from the shackles of his zip code.

Brandon pitched a rock at a water-stained wall. He rummaged through piles of rubble. The house looked like a remnant of postwar Europe. But for these boys it was a playground. Vandalism was something to do, an innocent pastime compared to drug dealing or murder.

"Them boys need Jesus." That's what the neighbor lady said of the young kids running around the block. "Else they goin' to hell or jail." These are two common destinations for kids growing up on these streets.

Brandon reached past a decayed rat to pick up a picture frame. He examined the portrait of a white family. Just then, a siren blared from the street. The boys ran for the back window. His colleague made it first. Brandon reached for the windowsill. He pushed down to launch himself when he felt an unbearable pain.

A rusty nail tore into his left hand. He saw the flashing glow of red light from the police car. Empowered by adrenaline, he ripped his hand from the nail. Blood traveled down his arm. The only thought in his mind was *Momma gonna kill me*. He feared his mother more than the police.

A black kid from these streets is bound to the gravitational pull of his context. Brandon was tied to circumstance and statistics. He was tethered to the issues of race, family upbringing, economics, and an educational achievement gap. His odds were tilted toward a predetermined destiny. "Them boys goin' to hell or jail," is what the old lady said as they ran down the alley.

Trespassing could have led to fatal vices had Brandon not jumped into a 15-passenger van the next week. He was on the street corner with some cousins, tossing rocks at a rusted-out car. The van approached the curb, and two of his cousins jumped in.

The door of the van read BETHLEHEM LUTHERAN CHURCH. It taxied kids from the neighborhood to an after-school program on Wednesdays. The old church gymnasium was a haven from alley fights and dope dealing at the neighborhood playground. Snacks, games, mentors, and learning took the place of unsupervised disorder.

Brandon stared at the open door to the van. "You gonna get in?" called the man behind the wheel. Brandon didn't know that getting in the van would be getting out of an old life.

Bethlehem is the name of the church on Salisbury Avenue in the Hyde Park neighborhood of St. Louis, Missouri. The congregation was named after the birthplace of a boy come to redeem every girl and boy. They call him the Son of God. And so it began for Brandon. A son of the streets redeemed from "hell or jail."

. . .

*And in Jesus Christ, His only Son, our Lord, who was conceived by
the Holy Spirit, born of the Virgin Mary, suffered under Pontius
Pilate, was crucified, died, and was buried. He descended into
hell. The third day He rose again from the dead. He ascended into
heaven and sits at the right hand of God, the Father Almighty.
From thence He will come to judge the living and the dead.*
—The Apostles' Creed

As Jacob listened to Ava, he heard inaccuracies in her description of Jesus. It wasn't her fault. She was echoing the Jesus she heard from the few Christians she knew. Many will paint a picture of a great moral teacher. A political revolutionary. A spiritual guru. Or an accidental hero.

Jacob held to the Christian belief that Jesus of Nazareth is true God and true man. Incarnation describes this mysterious confluence: *God in the flesh.* As God, he has the power to heal, restore, and die for sins. As man, he is able to fully identify with the gritty plight of human circumstance.

Ava was trying to make sense of the cruel and complex events of life. We all are. Christians are quick to respond, "Jesus is the answer!" But who is Jesus? Why is he the answer? Ava and those like her aren't satisfied with a thoughtless cliché. They deserve a substantive answer.

Too often, we are incapable of giving a compelling response to the questions surrounding the man from Nazareth. There seem to be as many answers as there are people on the planet. Was he a sage? A philosopher? A social activist? In an age of tolerance, anyone's opinion of Jesus is accepted as valid. Therefore, anyone can be an expert in misinformation.

Three simple objects give us the answer to who Jesus truly is: **a manger, a cross, and a crown.** They correspond to his life, death, and resurrection. They also follow the classic description of Jesus as prophet, priest, and King.

These three objects provide an explicit picture of the person and work of Jesus. In them, we see a love so vast that it moved God to send his Son so far.

MANGER: PRESENCE

Even in an interconnected, global society, loneliness and isolation are pervasive. It's common to feel disconnected and forgotten in a busy crowd. A teenager glued to his phone in a crowd of friends still wonders, *Who will be there for me? Does anyone understand me? Am I on my own?*

From the beginning God designed humans for an intimate existence—with himself and with one another. God gave Adam a perfect "fit" in Eve so that he wouldn't be alone (Gen. 2:18). God was so close to the first humans that he spoke to them directly (Gen. 1:28). There's even the sense that God took on a physical presence in the Garden of Eden as he strolled through his creation: "They heard the sound of the LORD God walking in the garden" (Gen. 3:8).

Although created for community, we now live with the grim reality of **separation.** Adam and Eve "hid themselves from the presence of the LORD God" (Gen. 3:8). Instead of joyfully walking in the presence of God, we hide in the bushes. We often feel alienated and abandoned. We are distant from God. And we are distant from others, even those we love.

God's response to separation is symbolized by a simple yet odd detail of Jesus' birth. The infant boy was placed in a **manger** instead of a proper crib (Luke 2:7,12,16). A manger is an animal feed box. Its contents are typically grain, hay, and cattle drool. The divine Son of God was not born in a sanitary delivery room, removed from risk and grit. His first nursery was a barn of sorts, a home for cattle.

This simple detail of Jesus' birth conveys a profound truth. The manger means that Jesus is **present with us.** The manger points to the mystery of the incarnation, the God who takes on flesh, even to the point of being born in a barn. He is not repulsed by our mess. Nor is he far removed from our experience. John wrote, "The Word became flesh and made his dwelling among us" (John 1:14).

The incarnation of Jesus means that God is not distant, but **near.** It means that he comes *to be with you,* even when you're not pleasant to be around. He enters difficult situations *and stays.* God does not avoid the messy and complicated. *He dwells right in the middle of it.* God is not absent, hiding in the remote recesses of heaven. He comes to us just as we are, even when we are not as we should be.

CROSS: PARDON

Guilty. Ashamed. Unworthy. Trapped. Remorseful. Every human wrestles with these feelings. They are evidence of the bruised human condition. The fundamental meaning of the Hebrew word for "sin" in the Old Testament is to "miss the mark." On a regular basis, we are left feeling like we've messed up and missed the target completely.

If any Christian says that he or she is perfect, they're delusional. Paul wrote in the Bible, "There is no one righteous, not even one; there is no one who understands, no one who seeks God. All have turned away, they have together become worthless; there is no one who does good, not even one" (Rom. 3:10–12). We submit to the sober assessment that we are not as good as we thought we were. Sin is serious.

In the Bible, sin is often talked about as a "debt." You spent something and now you owe. You're indebted. And like compound interest, sin grows exponentially. Every false word or selfish intention. Every lie or misuse of your body. It all adds up to an unbearable burden that you can never pay off.

God cannot ignore sin. When his goodness is violated, there must be payment. The universe is embedded with a basic sense of justice. Every wrong demands a sentence. Justice has to be maintained. With every misdeed, the debt continues to grow.

But in our overwhelming debt, God did something strange. When his justice demanded payment, God took the sentence upon himself. Our crimes, from the petty to the worst felonies, are pardoned. Sin is not simply dismissed. Rather, the consequence is redirected to another.

God counters our sin, not with castigation, but with a cross. A **cross** was a cruel form of capital punishment practiced by the Roman government in the first century. It was a slow, public, and humiliating form of execution. It was intended to crush rebellion and deter future revolt.

Jesus' punishment by crucifixion was not an unfortunate accident, as if he were in the wrong place at the wrong time. This execution had divine purpose. Centuries before Jesus, the prophet Isaiah articulated an unconventional form of clemency: "He was pierced for our transgressions, he was crushed for our iniquities; the punishment that brought us peace was on him, and by his wounds we are healed" (Is. 53:5).

Isaiah described a trade of sorts. One man would take on the transgressions of many. He would carry the consequence of our misdeeds. In return, we receive his innocence and peace. By this death, God pardons the collective debt amassed by humanity.

In the cruelty of the cross, we see God's heart to forgive. When I'm haunted by the past, the cross means pardon for what I cannot change. When there is no "redo," the cross means a clean slate. When I'm in the wrong, the cross of Christ declares me right. When I'm trapped by guilt, the cross means substitution—his life for mine; his death in my place, for my sins.

To this day, cross-shaped gallows have been erected around the world in honor of this man's death. On steeples, necklaces, and tattooed on skin—the cross remains the raw symbol of pardon's price.

CROWN: POWER

We fear words like "foreclosure," "inoperable," or "terminal." We are regularly confronted by our weakness and frailty. There are circumstances beyond our control. Our best-laid plans are upended. Failure, frustration, and chaos rule an average day.

One of the consequences of our sinful world is a sense that we are *powerless.* Our powerlessness is evident when we feel oppressed, weak, or incompetent. We realize our limitations when we are sick or addicted. Our mortality is ultimate evidence of our frailty, undeniable proof of our powerlessness.

Jesus was crucified. It was a most powerless position. Buried in a grave, his fate seemed no different than any of ours . . . until he was seen alive by hundreds of witnesses. The Roman government and the religious authorities were unable to find his body. Cemetery guards were paid to claim his body was stolen.

As Christians, we hold to the bold assertion that Jesus of Nazareth rose from the dead and now stands as the risen King of the entire universe. The cross gave way to a crown, grief to glory, tragedy to victory. Christians to this day speak of Jesus Christ in the *present tense.* He *is* alive.

The crown is symbolic of the **resurrection power** of God. The word "resurrection" literally means, "to stand again." It is the ultimate act of God's recreating power. For centuries Christian headstones were inscribed with the Latin term *resurgam,* which means, "I shall rise." All those in Christ follow his pattern of death and resurrection. We believe that on the Last Day, our bodies will rise, new and imperishable (I Cor. 15). We were created body and soul. Death rips that union in two. Resurrection restores us to whole people again, living and breathing.

Resurrection tells us that our God is a God of life. It means that in loss, God works victory. It means that history is steadily advancing toward a powerful Last Day of resurrection, a new heavens and a new earth. It means everything will be fully set right under the merciful rule of the crucified and risen one.

The crown not only has eternal consequence, but it also means that Jesus rules *presently.* "He ascended into heaven and sits at the right hand of God, the Father Almighty." This fact gives us motivation for present-day living. We believe Jesus Christ to be the risen, mighty, universal, worldwide King over all powers and principalities. In spite of the brokenness we may see, all is not lost. Failure is not the final result. Living under the rule of an active King gives us reason to live out our lives with zeal and passion.

This fact is especially empowering when we're faced with impossible circumstances. In the cross and crown we find that God has a way of working power in the most desperate moments. Jesus said to Paul, "My grace is sufficient for you, for my power is made perfect in weakness" (II Corinthians 12:9). We anticipate God's power in feeble weakness. In the most hellish valleys, God flexes his muscle.

• • •

My wife spent over a decade teaching at Lift for Life Academy, an urban junior high and high school. One day, a boy made inappropriate comments about a classmate's mother. Bobbi was so fed up that she hauled the young man to the office and called his mom.

"Yes, your son has something to say to you," she said, and handed the phone to the perpetrator.

"Hello . . . Momma?" he mumbled.

"Tell your mom what you said in class," Bobbi demanded.

The boy was horrified. Bobbi gave him the death stare until he quietly spoke into the phone. After a pause, Momma's rebuke could be heard throughout the office. It was like the phone was on speaker. "YOU SAID WHAT?!"

Bobbi witnessed the triumphs and tragedies of urban education. There is an emotional toll in watching kids stuck in devastating patterns. It hurts to see young men repeat the sins of their absent fathers. It's depressing to see a 13-year-old arrested, a 15-year-old pregnant, or a senior drop out of high school.

"Them boys need Jesus," is what Brandon's neighbor lady said. "Else they goin' to hell or jail." For years, I've wrestled with the plight of our urban communities. I've come to realize that suburbs and small towns also have their own forms of poverty. We are mistaken if we think that sin is relegated to certain people and zip codes. Money and morality cloak a wealth of darkness. Disobedience is everywhere and inside everyone. Some of us are just better at covering it up.

The point is that sin is an egalitarian enterprise. We are all practiced in its deviant ways. We are all shackled by its chain. The only solution is a radical love. The credentials of this love are the manger, cross, and crown of Jesus. Here we see that love is more than mere sentiment.

Christ's identity is a validation of my own identity. His presence with me. His pardon for me. His power over me. The costly mission of Jesus alters my living and being. My destiny is not "hell or jail." It's *loved* and *sent*.

Reflect

> There are a variety of opinions about Jesus in our culture. List a few common perceptions of Jesus Christ.

> How can the manger be especially good news to someone who is alone? An orphan? A person suffering from depression?

> We have tamed the scandal of the cross, a device for execution. How does the raw reality of a criminal's death reveal God's love to an even greater degree? Read I John 4:7.

> How is the crown especially good news for those who are suffering injustice? Grieving the loss of a loved one?

> Someone asks you, "Who do you think Jesus is?" How does "manger, cross, crown" help you formulate a clear, concise, consistent, and compelling response?

HOLY SPIRIT

Her voice, dignified by its British accent, called to me down the church hallway. I anticipated the old lady's rebuke. I had snickered with some friends during the sex education video. What do you expect from 12-year-old boys? The animated cartoon buttocks begged us to giggle.

"Jeffrey, come with me," she said. Kay Johnson, or "Lady Kay," grew up in England during the Second World War. As our Sunday school teacher, she told us childhood stories of hiding in bomb shelters. She recounted the fear incited by the sirens. After the war, she married Bill, an American soldier. They retreated to his hometown in the remote woods of northern Michigan.

Lady Kay was a graceful woman. Her white hair refused to obey gravity's command. It rose upward in a wave above her forehead. She was eccentric by the standards of our small town. Lady Kay didn't operate by convention. Norms and rules were recognized but not always obeyed.

There are people who believe *in* God, and then there are people who *believe* God. Lady Kay anticipated God's activity in ordinary moments of mundane life. Jesus said, "Ask, seek, and knock." So Kay would plead and pound, expecting God's response. She didn't just pray—*she spoke with God.* Her faith earned her immense authority in my young eyes.

I'm just a kid. This is what I often thought to myself. As a boy I experienced moments of humiliation and feelings of uselessness. Children are often dismissed, to be seen and not heard. Adults are supposed to discipline children. Keep them in order. Lady Kay set me aside that day, not to scold but to empower.

"Jeffrey, I saw your Little League game yesterday," she said, her dignified accent turning this lecture into a queen's speech.

"Yeah?"

"You wear the number seven. It's prominent on the back of your jersey. Do you know why that's significant?"

"Uh . . . no."

"Seven is a holy number. It's the number of completeness. You're a special boy, Jeffrey."

I doubted that. But she proceeded, and I dared not contradict Lady Kay. "God will use you mightily, Jeffrey. You will speak for him."

She didn't talk like a teacher or parent. She spoke like a prophetess. She saw things most people couldn't. I felt like a useless boy. She believed an alternative reality. Her belief about me was peculiar. *I was empowered to do something for God?*

I walked back to the chatter of my friends with their gossip and giggling. At that moment, I sensed something different about life. Every moment was filled with possibility. Not of my own making, but of holy initiative. Can people change? Do miracles happen? Are there such things as holy surprises? Can God do extraordinary things when life seems so ordinary?

"You will speak for God," she said. As I write these words, I think of Lady Kay.

. . .

I believe in the Holy Spirit, the holy Christian Church,
the communion of saints, the forgiveness of sins, the
resurrection of the body, and the life everlasting.
—The Apostles' Creed

Ava had a valid critique. She expounded upon her experience of self-righteous and arrogant religious people. Christians claim holiness, but they clearly aren't holy. Those who claim to follow Jesus often look nothing like him. What does that say about their faith?

On our best days, we valiantly aim to live good and God-pleasing lives. But for Christians, even our greatest moments seem to lack something. We still feel that we haven't done all that we can or should. Or worse, we find that we've made a royal mess of things.

Lady Kay recognized the need for a bandwidth beyond normal human capacity. She lived with a sincere attentiveness to a power beyond herself. She saw a need for something truly holy because she knew that she was not.

To those who are weak and inadequate, to the useless and powerless, to the sorry sinner, **Jesus sends the Spirit of God.** He said, "But very truly I tell you, it is for your good that I am going away. Unless I go away, the Advocate will not come to you; but if I go, I will send him to you" (John 16:7). To fully be the people God longs for us to be, we need more than our best intentions. We need a divine Helper.

Martin Luther commented on the third article of the Creed, "I believe that I cannot by my own reason or strength believe in Jesus Christ . . . but the Holy Spirit has called me by the Gospel . . ." On the one hand, we suffer the frail limitations of our own "reason" and "strength." On the other hand, we believe that the Holy Spirit has the capacity to do what we are unable to accomplish.

As much as we acknowledge our own weakness, we believe even more in the powerful working of God. To believe in God is to believe in the power of his Spirit, the third person of the Trinity, true God with the Father and the Son.

The Holy Spirit does the supernatural work of sanctification, "making holy" in order to transform, enlighten and empower us. There is a dual nature to this "making holy." God works *in* and *through* us. As we relate to God, the Spirit works *in* us to nurture a relationship with him. In regard to our fellow human beings, the Spirit works *through* us in our service and witness to the world.

Here are some key characteristics of the Spirit who works *in* and *through* us.

THE SPIRIT *IN* US

The Holy Spirit is a **connector.** The Spirit works *in* us to connect us to God. Why can't we connect on our own? The cancerous nature of sin is so tangled around our heart that for all our best efforts, we are incapable of perfectly loving or trusting God. So tainted is our conscience that we need an invasive procedure, a force from outside ourselves.

From this desperate position, King David cried out, "Do not cast me from your presence or take your Holy Spirit from me" (Ps. 51:11). The posture exhibited by David is one of self-awareness and transparency. We admit that our own spirits are faulty and fickle. We need a "pouring out" of the Spirit of God in the vessel of our empty hearts (Is. 44:3; Joel 2:28; Acts 2:17). There is no room for arrogance or ego, just openness to a Helper.

In this deep need, **the Spirit creates and sustains faith within us.** He works powerfully, often behind the scenes, pointing and connecting people to Christ. Jesus said, "He will glorify me because it is from me that he will receive what he will make known to you" (John 16:14). By connecting us to Jesus, the "Spirit gives life" (John 6:63; II Cor. 3:6) where there was once only a dead heart.

This is good news for us when we doubt our connection to God. There are days when we wake up and don't *feel* very Christian. We need more than superficial help. The Holy Spirit has the capability to invade the depths of heart and mind. The Spirit rounds the rough edges of our brazen will and restless soul. He overcomes our whims and weaknesses. He conforms our hearts and minds to that of God.

Sometimes the Holy Spirit works in wild and unexpected ways to connect with us. A disciple named Philip was sent to an Ethiopian who had questions about God. By the power of the Spirit, Philip told him the good news about Jesus, and then was supernaturally carried away (Acts 8:39). Some of us have such extraordinary stories of conversion.

At the same time, the Holy Spirit works through plain and ordinary things. For instance, the Spirit shows up in water at baptism (John 3:5; Acts 2:38–39) or in the word of God when it is proclaimed (Acts 10:44). We dare not dismiss the ordinary ways that the Spirit of God works. We call these "means of grace." They are the subtle and surprising means by which the Holy Spirit connects us to God.

It's important to know that the Holy Spirit often leads us into challenge and difficulty. The Spirit once led Jesus into the desert for 40 days of testing and temptation by the devil (Matt. 4:1). The fact that the Spirit leads us into contested territory runs contrary to a popular belief that the Spirit only brings blessing and happiness. The Spirit's work in us can be startling, even troubling, as we are tested by trials (Deut. 13:3; Jas. 1:3).

Yet God never leaves us to face confrontation alone. We are led into testing, and there we find the Spirit to be our Helper and Comforter (John 14:26). We are led into places of vulnerability and temptation. In the midst of struggle, the Spirit helps us stand firm and calls us to trust only in God (Eph. 3:16). Such times of testing grow us. In this way the Holy Spirit works in us to nurture an ever-deepened faith.

God's people face pressure daily. The Holy Spirit stands as the Defender of God's Word and his people. He gives faith to believers and empowers them to stand firmly in that faith. Paul writes of the "sword of the Spirit," a weapon and sure defense against all danger (Eph. 6:17). Possessed by the very Spirit of the Living God, trembling hearts are made brave. The timid are given the ability to "speak the word of God boldly" (Acts 4:31). This is the Holy Spirit *in* us.

THE SPIRIT *THROUGH* US

Just as the Spirit of God works *in* us, he also works *through* us. We are more than sorry souls that need saving. We are repurposed for divine work. Sinners become saints in the hands of God, and he uses them for his purpose in the world.

That God would conscript *us* for holy service is scandalous. We feel anything but holy. So the Holy Spirit gets to work. The Spirit of God is the great **Transformer,** changing us from one person into another, from old to new. He enlightens and empowers us to lead a godly life. The Spirit works in us to renew our whole lives—in spirit, will, attitude, and behavior.

In this way, we become more and more the men and women God would have us be. Our self-centered inclinations are challenged as the Spirit reshapes us to live out God's intentions in the world. Such transformation is a process, and at times a painful one. Old patterns and desires are dismantled. New, life-giving ways are imposed.

Paul wrote about the "fruit of the Spirit" (Gal. 5:22–23) and the gifts of the Spirit "for the common good" (I Cor. 12:7). In theory, attributes like "love, joy, peace, and patience" sound desirable. Yet to enact them in the daily trials of life is a heroic feat. Thus the Holy Spirit bestows a supernatural capacity to live in God's ways. Only by the transformation of the Spirit can we increasingly reflect the "goodness" that the Creator intended from the beginning.

As the Holy Spirit works *through* us *for* others, our lives take on holy purpose. We authentically bear spiritual fruit. Our love and work become good for families, neighbors, and friends. We are agents of God's will in the world.

The Spirit also works through us as witnesses. "Who is God?" In each generation, he uses people to reveal his identity. Through his people, he is known. The Holy Spirit animates his people to bold witness of the Gospel. Here the Spirit is the subject of the verb "sent." In stunning ways, the Spirit sends people as carriers of the Gospel (Acts 10:20; 13:4).

Early in the book of Acts, the disciples of Jesus were few in number. Additionally, they had moments of fear and timidity after Jesus' crucifixion (John 20:19). In the wake of their leader's death, uncertainty proved to be a crippling force. In spite of their fear, this tattered band of followers received a power beyond their own capacity (Acts 1:8). At the Pentecost event, the Spirit empowered the disciples to speak boldly (in various languages) to their hope in Christ (Acts 2:4). Unqualified and ordinary, these first Christians advanced with courage and bravery.

The numbers of the early church are fascinating. Jesus began with 12 (Mark 3:13–19). At one point, he sent out 72 followers in pairs (Luke 10:1–12). Though masses followed him throughout his ministry, only 120 counted themselves disciples after his tragic death (Acts 1:15). Christianity appeared to be a short-lived fad. But at the instigation of the Holy Spirit, the number radically jumped to 3,000 in one day (Acts 2:41).

From that point a movement rapidly swept across the Mediterranean world and beyond (Acts 1:8). Scholars continue to study the viral phenomenon called the "early church." This global movement now numbers in the billions across every continent. Sociological factors are often cited. Christians cite the Holy Spirit.

Even with the Spirit's supernatural work, Christians don't claim perfection. We assert a paradox. "We are saints and sinners at the same time," we confess. Saints by God's work in us. Sinners by our core propensity to regress to our selfish nature. We are continually a work in progress. It's a wonder that God doesn't scrap such a messy people. Even still, his Spirit keeps working *in* and *through*. We pray, "Come, Holy Spirit, come."

. . .

If you live in the Upper Peninsula of Michigan, you're called a Yooper. The
U.P. is the forgotten territory of Michigan. Much of its land is remote.
Yoopers possess a unique culture and set of customs. School is suspended
for a week during deer season. The pasty is a dietary staple: meat and
potatoes buried in the center of a bread crust. The Yooper accent is distinct,
and most sentences end in an "eh?" Like, "Nice day out, eh?"

With her wisp of white hair and British accent, Lady Kay was an oddity
among her Yooper neighbors. As the prophets of old would stick out from
their surrounding culture, Lady Kay was a distinguished woman. Although
she could leave you confused, the Spirit worked in and through her to bless
many. Lady Kay was a walking witness for her God.

Who is God? He stands out from the marketplace of gods and self-help
gurus. Like Lady Kay among the Yoopers, this God is unlike any other. He is
not distant or generic. He is personal and particular. In his very essence, he
reveals himself as relational. One God in three persons. Father. Son. Spirit.

Many people like Lady Kay helped me on my journey to know God. As
I came to know who he was, I began to know who I was. I thought I was a
forgettable kid from the remote recesses of northern Michigan. But Lady
Kay said, "You're a special boy. You will speak for God." Years later, I look
back and hear, "You are loved more than you can imagine. You're sent with
more purpose than you thought." I'm grateful for that Yooper prophetess
with a British accent and a wisp of white hair.

Reflect

> Do you think that most Christians would agree with Martin Luther's sober assessment that "I cannot by my own reason or strength believe in Jesus Christ?" Why or why not?
> Has there been a time when the Holy Spirit worked in your life in an extraordinary way? How about an ordinary way?
> We believe that the Holy Spirit is working through us. How does this give your life more purpose?
> We often feel inadequate and unqualified to do God's work. How does a belief in the Spirit's power address that fear?

TWO

WHO AM I?

I was rumored to be 6'8", 230 lbs. It was whispered in the school hallways that I was a hoops phenom from Detroit. Duke, North Carolina, and Kentucky were all recruiting me. Gossip grew into myth, and I had a shoe deal with Nike and an agent in L.A. I was a new kid, moving to a new high school during the summer after my sophomore year. And my legend grew, *all before the student body had ever met me.*

The legend fizzled when they discovered reality. I was a skinny white kid, standing 6'3". I was from the state of Michigan, but not the urban playgrounds of Detroit. I was from Bessemer, a remote logging town nestled in the rugged hills of the Upper Peninsula. Was I a hoops phenom? I possessed moderate skills. I had enough to make varsity but certainly not to dominate.

They say that where you're from is part of who you are. What happens when you're not from anywhere? I departed my small boyhood town with a class of 30. I arrived in central Minnesota to a class of hundreds. I knew no one. I left everything that made me *me.* Friends and familiarity. A place

I knew and that knew me. A sense of belonging. "Who am I now?" I wondered.

I spent the summer playing 76 games of cribbage with my brother, John, and learning how to dunk. After boredom turned to depression, I got a job washing dishes at a Mexican restaurant. I spent hours chiseling hardened cheese off of plates. I listened to stoned coworkers mumble nonsense. As each day of summer passed, my anxiety for the first day of school grew.

It is human nature to find our identity in what we can do, show, build, or prove. So we strive to be pretty, popular, or productive. At that moment, I only felt vulnerable and irrelevant. *Does anyone understand me? Is there anyone willing to sit with me when I'm worthless?*

My first day at Sauk Rapids High School was marked by sweaty armpits and the feeling of a wrench in my gut. I glanced at unfamiliar faces as I roamed the endless hallways hunting for my locker. The school had the sterile scent of newly waxed floors and Windex. I found number 207 and fumbled with the lock for a minute. Frustration came at 60 seconds. Fear emerged at two minutes. *What if I never open this locker all year?*

A sturdy-looking kid in a football jersey approached me. I pretended to know what I was doing. He wasn't fooled. "Let me show you the trick." He jiggled and pounded the lock. It opened and I said, "Thank you."

At lunchtime, I found one of the few empty tables and sat alone. I was about to bite into my sandwich when the same kid in the football jersey spotted me. "Sit by us," he said. I collected my lunch and thought, *Maybe I'm okay.* I sat with him and a table full of future friends.

• • •

In a new town I discovered new aspects of my identity and purpose. It was like starting life over again. Rather than a curse, I began to see purpose in a high school move. I didn't just haphazardly end up in a new place. *I was sent there.* And in the sending, my understanding of God's love increased.

By 16, I knew the Bible and all the stories. But I had to ask, "What does this have to do with *me*? How does it become *my* story? Am *I* loved? Am *I* sent? What about the first day of school in the cafeteria?

For every Christian, there exists a point where **who God is** intersects with **who I am**. His transcendent work is mere history or philosophy unless it somehow invades the present and personal. So the followers of Jesus mark points where *God's* story becomes *their* story. This mighty God who worked wonders of old is *my* God, working in *my* life and time.

Because of who God is, I know who I am. *I am a beloved child of God.* This fact is quickly forgotten throughout the stress of a day. Therefore God's love is continually expressed. It is not static, but dynamic. Here are three elements that define my God-given identity. This is how I know who I am. This is where I go when I forget. Grace. Word. Community.

GRACE

His body was a shell, slouched and captive in a chair. His tongue could not move to form words. His cheeks could not stretch into a smile. On the inside, George's mind was active with thoughts, feelings, and fears. From the outside, the only observable movement was the darting of his eyes.

When I first met George Richardson, he was in an early stage of ALS, or Lou Gehrig's Disease. It's a mysteriously wicked disease that immobilizes the nervous system. Like a slow shipwreck, the body is dismantled piece by piece.

Early on we discussed coins. As an avid collector, George's favorite was the Stone Mountain silver half-dollar. It displays a portrait of Robert E. Lee and Stonewall Jackson on the face. It is named after Stone Mountain in Georgia where a sculpture of the Confederate legends exists.

From then on, I called George "Mr. Stone Mountain." He was always cordial, but with a gruff strength. His life experiences forged him into a rock. As a boy, he worked farms in southeast Missouri. He served his country as a Marine through four years of active duty with deployments to

Hong Kong and Okinawa. He was a loyal employee of a freight company for 30 years.

But Mr. Stone Mountain began to crack when he was diagnosed with ALS at age 65. George's life changed rapidly. As his strength and independence slipped away, his loving wife, Judy, had to care for his every need.

George was not a religious man. His wife and daughter were fervent in their Christian faith. George was respectful, but personally indifferent to God. "That's fine for you, but it's not for me. I'm okay on my own." Mr. Stone Mountain had faith in the persistent strength of the human will. To believe in God, for George, was to demean his own strength and dignity.

This is what made the disease particularly cruel for George. ALS eventually stripped him of all he believed was true. The man who once did everything himself now needed someone to bathe him and trim his toenails.

Shortly after a tracheotomy, Judy and I sat by George's bedside. Many people had "God conversations" with George, but it was getting more serious now. Judy would often converse with him about the afterlife, sin, regret, and Jesus.

I asked George, "Mr. Stone Mountain, what do you think of Jesus?" We had talked about the manger, cross, and crown of Christ. He was curious about presence, pardon, and power. But the conversation usually drifted back to coins, sports, and current events. This particular conversation was different.

There was a pride in George that made grace incomprehensible. "There's no such thing as a free lunch," they say. You have to earn it. This is our common belief about life.

I rephrased my question over the hum and hiss of the ventilator. "George, do you want Jesus?" He labored to communicate. "I'm ashamed to want God's help now. I've stayed away for 68 years."

"George, he hasn't given up on you," I replied.

"I've pushed him away."

"But he never left."

He still doubted. "I don't deserve God now. Not when I'm like this." He repeated, "Not now, when I'm like this."

I countered, "You're right. But God has a way of giving what we don't deserve. He still wants you, George. Even now. Just as you are."

After a moment of silence, a tear on his cheek stunned me. Mr. Stone Mountain, tough as a rock, was cracking. A flow of tears commenced. "I want help," he whispered with all the lung capacity he could muster. "I want Jesus."

That day George had communion for the first time. The sacred meal instituted by Jesus had a new guest at the table. A little piece of bread on his tongue. "This is Jesus' body for you." Then came the wine. He couldn't swallow, so his wife Judy retrieved a small sponge on the end of a stick. I dipped it into the wine and touched it to his tongue. "This is the blood of Christ, shed for you." More tears ensued.

Life only got harder for George as the days passed. There were times of terrifying uncertainty in his mind. Yet there was also a spirit of intense hope that trudged through the shadowy valley of death.

I was with George the day he died two years later. With two hours left in his earthly life, we had communion one last time. His wife, daughter, and son-in-law huddled around the bed in his room. We squeezed between the machines that were keeping him alive. They would soon be switched off.

As I was preparing the bread and wine, Judy handed me a discolored object. It was a ratty old sponge. "What's this?" I asked. "It's the one from the first time he had communion," she explained. So we shared this meal once more. In his broken body, George had one last taste before he would meet his Lord face to face.

I think of George with regularity. The Stone Mountain silver dollar he gave me is on my shelf. I think of the new life he's living at this moment, life with the Lord he resisted for so long. George wasn't a perfectly pious super-saint. But he was loved by God even when he didn't love God back. There is a term for his kind of undeserved favor. We call it *grace.*

. . .

The religions of the world are all about humans reaching up to the divine. Even Ava's atheism is an attempt to achieve something sublime, even if only for this lifetime. In Islam, it is rigid obedience to the Five Pillars. In Buddhism, enlightenment comes by your effort on the Eightfold Path. Even some Christians turn Christianity into a religion of rule-following. "If I just obey the Ten Commandments . . . if I'm just a good person . . . if I just go to church."

If life is like drowning in a pool, most religions beckon us to get ourselves out. They provide the ladder or floatation device, but you must find the edge and pull yourself up. There are three general ways in which humans reach for God, regardless of their religion (or lack of religion).

Human will: Moral living. Doing the right thing. ("I'm a good person." "I follow the rules.")

Human intellect: Special knowledge. Knowing the right thing. ("I have understanding.")

Human experience: Feelings and emotions. Experiencing the right thing. ("I feel the supernatural." "I am spiritual.")

Christianity takes human will, intellect, and experience into account. The distinctive difference is the insistence that **God takes the initiative** in his relationship with us. Any Christian preacher who says, "you have to get right to get in" has missed the most fundamental component of Christianity. Central to the Christian faith is the astounding nature of *God's action over human effort.*

Note again that the word "loved" is a passive word. To be loved is to be the recipient of another's care and affection. A key Biblical word expounds on the nature of this love: grace.

Grace is unmerited favor. It is an undeserved gift bestowed on one who didn't earn it. It is goodness shown to another with no conditions or obligations. Grace knows the harsh reality that humans cannot reach up to the divine. So the divine reaches down to humanity.

God's grace is made explicit in the manger, cross, and crown of Jesus. In his manger, God drew near, though humanity pushed him away. In his cross, God took the punishment we deserved. In his crown, he gave life when we were dead. What our effort could never accomplish, God did for us (Rom. 9:16; Eph. 2:8–9).

Why does grace matter? I have seen too many people damaged by religion. If my relationship with God were completely dependent on my résumé, my credentials would disqualify me. If salvation were based on my performance, the curtain would have closed a long time ago. If faith were based on a strict morality, I would be crushed by the burden of living up to an unreachable standard.

Any religious foundation based on human will, knowledge, or experience leads down one of two dangerous roads. The first road is arrogance. I can become self-righteous. "Look what I've done. Look how good I am." The second road is despair. In trying to be good I discover that I'm never good enough. "God will never take me."

We all try to prove ourselves by creating an identity worth keeping. Society values those who are productive and profitable. Like a child we shout, "Look at me! Look what I can do!" What we really mean by this plea is, "Love me! Respect me! Admire me! Accept me!"

Grace says, "No. You are loved apart from the great things you can do." More than that, you are loved *in spite of* the worst things that you've done. This is good news for weary people exhausted by failed attempts at reaching an unattainable bar. Ruined by my vain pursuits, I rest in the reality that I'm under God's grace.

LAW AND GOSPEL

During the sixteenth century, a monk named Martin Luther challenged some of the teachings and practices of the Roman Catholic Church. He insisted that the church had gotten off track and compromised the central message of Christianity: sinners are reconciled to God by grace through faith because of the saving work of Jesus Christ.

Luther identified *"solas"* (Latin for "only" or "alone") as a means to refocus the church on the heart of its faith. God is not overly impressed by our will, intellect, or experience. Our acceptance is by *grace alone,* through *faith alone,* informed by *Scripture alone.*

In a struggle for true, authentic Christianity, Luther returned to the source: the Holy Scriptures. In doing so, he described a recurring distinction found throughout the Biblical text. He labeled it Law and Gospel.

Law and Gospel convey a profound truth about God and life. The truth is this: **we are worse than we thought, and God is greater than we imagined.** The Law reveals the sobering truth that we are worse. The Gospel shows God's goodness in spite of our worst.

The Law is the perfect will of God. It is the picture of what is right and true. It was established at creation, spelled out in the Ten Commandments (Ex. 20) and fulfilled by Jesus (Matt. 5:17). The problem is that the perfection of the Law only magnifies our imperfection. It shows our sin, the inability of humans to be who they are supposed to be.

The Law is like staring at a perfect physical specimen. As I look at him, I compare myself. Immediately my flaws come into focus. My blemishes and scars are obvious. Wrinkles and flab are exposed. In a similar way, the Law makes our imperfections undeniably evident.

This is where the Gospel comes in. If the Law shows our sin, the Gospel shows our Savior. If the Law shows us the depth of our need, the Gospel shows us the depth of God's grace. If the Law exposes the severity of our condition, the Gospel reveals the splendid tenderness of God's heart. Luther writes, "While the Law says 'do this,' and it is never done, Grace says 'believe in this,' and everything is already done."

Why does this matter? Law and Gospel allow me to be incredibly honest. Winston Churchill once said, "A clear conscience is the sign of a fuzzy memory." There is absolutely no room for hypocritical self-righteousness.

I am worse than I thought. Having admitted this outright, I don't have to cover up or hide. God knows the truth about me, the truth that I don't even want to admit to myself.

But right at this moment, a second and greater truth is spoken. It's the truth of what God says about me in spite of the first truth. I'm worse, *but he's better.* I'm a mess, but he doesn't look away. I'm a wreck, but he doesn't leave. He delivers me by a mercy that is just as severe as my sin. This is the Gospel.

In medical terms, if you're sick, you want to know the truth about your illness. You don't want it sugarcoated. The Law shows us the honest reality of our sickened condition. The doctor doesn't hold back. "It doesn't look good."

But a true diagnosis leads us to an unbelievable remedy. The Gospel is the salve applied to our most traumatic wounds. The remedy was procured at a high cost. Only by the blood of God's Son are we healed. A terminal diagnosis is reversed in Jesus Christ.

A Law and Gospel distinction is the lens through which we view our world. We are not alarmed by sin and evil, because we recognize the deep darkness we live in. Yet we do not despair, because we believe in the mercy of God in Jesus Christ. We recognize that we can't do enough, and we know Jesus has done it all. We admit the toxic nature of our sin, and we look only to our Savior.

RADICAL GRACE

George wrestled with God for years because grace is counterintuitive to the way we view life. We resist it for at least two reasons: First, pride doesn't like help or handouts. We want a reason to be blessed. We prefer to have earned and deserved it. Second, grace is an admission of need. Grace, by its nature, implies your inadequacy. You were wrong, weak, or untrue.

Someone once told me to write down as many blessings as I could in 90 seconds. Literally, take a notepad and fill it up with all the things you're grateful for. After you've filled up a page, look at the list. Consider the fact that you ultimately had nothing to do with obtaining these things. Yes, you may have worked hard. But every blessing can be traced back to a source beyond you. Blessings are gifts given. Some people call it luck, chance, or the fruit of hard work. We call it God's grace.

Grace is not only in effect on good days. Or when you have a saintly résumé. Or after you achieve success. Grace is good on your worst day. Your ugliest moment. When you had no good reason to be loved. That's exactly when grace proved true in the costly act of Jesus Christ. Paul makes the claim, "While we were still sinners, Christ died for us" (Rom. 5:8). God didn't require some moral threshold before saving us. He died for us when we were at our worst.

Grace exposes the extremities of God's love. I have yet to find a religion that has such a radical form of grace. There are elements of this concept in other religions (Mahayana Buddhism, for instance). Yet no worldview embraces such a selfless sense of love with no demands, obligations, or conditions. God's love sacrifices in the face of unexplainable circumstances.

You've been called a failure, a sinner, and an idiot. Grace is the strange disposition of God to call you someone else: beloved. And he calls you beloved precisely when you are unlovable. This is God's grace, expanding the boundaries of love beyond any horizon we've ever seen.

• • •

After George died, his wife, Judy, placed a rock in the garden near her backyard patio. It's called an "Ebenezer Stone." "Ebenezer" means "stone of help" (I Sam. 7:12). It reminds her of George, Mr. Stone Mountain. Even more, it is a miniature monument to a greater Rock.

Every Sunday is a good day for Judy, but it gets a lot better if we sing one particular hymn in worship. "Come Thou Fount" is an eighteenth-century hymn penned by Robert Robinson. It reminds her of God's grace for George. The second stanza is her favorite:

Here I raise my Ebenezer;
Here by Thy great help I've come;
And I hope, by Thy good pleasure,
Safely to arrive at home.
Jesus sought me when a stranger,
Wandering from the fold of God;
He, to rescue me from danger,
Interposed His precious blood.

Who am I? I am a man **loved by God.** Not because I'm so good, but because he's so gracious. Judy's Ebenezer stone is a monument to this truth. It reminds me that God's grace is good, even for Mr. Stone Mountain. Even for me.

Reflect

> In a culture that values productivity, achievement, and success, why is grace difficult to understand?

> Many people are turned off by what they perceive as a "holier than thou" attitude among Christians. How do Law and Gospel address self-righteousness?

> Romans 5:8 states, "But God demonstrates his own love for us in this: While we were still sinners, Christ died for us." Why is this a radical statement among religions founded on human will or intellect?

> Recount a moment when you most clearly experienced grace.

> As one who has received God's grace, how can you express his grace to someone else?

WORD

His name was Ottmar Helmut Cloeter. It's as stern and sturdy a name as the German language possesses. His name was like his face, a chiseled profile cast in stone. He was my grandfather, but I often wondered what was veiled behind the face. What does Grandpa think of me? Is he proud of me? Does he love me?

Ottmar bore the legacy of a stoic tribe of people. This Germanic heritage was furthered by the fact that he grew up in the Great Depression. Grandpa had a curious tick when he drank soda or beer from a can. With the can at his lip he would flip his head back in a series of rhythmic shakes. He had to retrieve every single drop of liquid. These are the peculiar habits formed by the Depression.

A day's journey would take us to Grandma and Grandpa's. As a child, I remember entering the front door. The smell of well-aged furniture. The clean and orderly home. The peanuts in the bowl on the counter. And Grandpa in his 1970s orange recliner.

He was always concealed by the newspaper. I wanted his attention, for my presence to be noticed. "Hi, Grandpa." He lowered the paper enough to make eye contact and respond, "Hello, Jeff." A cordial acknowledgement, but, like a wall, the newsprint rose again and his face disappeared.

Ask me about school, I pleaded in my mind. *Ask me about seventh-grade basketball. Ask me to come into your office and show me the treasures in your desk. Tell me about the wildest things you did as a kid.*

I was a young father when I saw Grandpa for the last time. Bobbi and I suffered through a nine-hour car ride with the kids. I remember a saturated diaper that seeped into the car seat. Grandma and Grandpa had recently moved to an assisted living facility. We tumbled out of the car and wearily walked up the stairs to their apartment. Exhausted and crabby, we put on smiles.

Hugs and pleasantries were exchanged. Grandma gave us her signature wet smooch that she called "a squeaker." I expected a moment to catch my breath on the couch. But Grandpa reported, "Well, it's time for Grandma and me to eat lunch in the cafeteria." Yes, it was 11:57, and the residents were assembling to eat downstairs. In my mind I screamed, "We came all this way to see you and you . . ." But I mustered, "We'll walk you down."

We huddled at their assigned table. My wife and children were a spectacle for the senior citizens awaiting their food. During this time, the mail was distributed to each resident. I expected a few more minutes of conversation, but Grandpa was fixated on his mail. He carefully opened each piece. A bill. A solicitation. A card from a friend. An ad. This was my last memory of Grandpa. Opening the mail while I was dismissed and ignored. I longed for him to speak, but no words came.

I believe Ottmar cared for me. But with frustration, I wondered why he didn't convey it. We are men, and we resist emotive disclosure. My father and I inherited the stoicism of our forefathers. Yet Dad broke the generational cycle.

I remember the conversation and the exact words spoken. My dad had said them before, but I don't clearly remember a moment like the phone call in college. It was a check-in that occurred every other week. Cell phones were not yet a mainstream commodity, so I picked up the landline and dialed the 1-800 number and the long-distance code.

We talked about necessary things. Tuition payments. How school was going. When I would be coming home next. Then the conversation began its conclusion.

"Well, I better go to class."

"Yeah, I'll let you go."

"Say hi to Mom."

"Will do."

"Okay."

"Alright."

"Well..."

"I love you, Jeff."

I paused for the gravity of these words. My dad had said, "I love you" before, throughout boyhood. But now he was speaking these words to an adult. I was on my own. "I love you" is a harder phrase to share man to man. When he said it, there was sincerity and power behind the words. "I love you too," I said, and hung up.

Today my dad and I live states apart, so we call each other every Friday. To this day, every phone conversation ends with the sure and certain words, "I love you."

• • •

Language is important. Words reveal what otherwise might be hidden. The truth may never be known but for a few words given a voice. There are words spoken that can't be taken back. And there are words unspoken that will never be heard. The right words, at the right time, can change your life.

Christianity is a religion of the word. God is a God whose word is action and event. He speaks, *and it is* (Gen. 1). All of Scripture is about God speaking—in his creation, to his people, through prophets, and ultimately by his Son (John 1:14; Heb. 1:2). Though the essence of the divine word transcends human linguistics, it is encapsulated and incarnated in language.

Who am I? It is common to look inside ourselves for validation. "Listen to your heart." "Find your inner voice." "Discover your true self." We whisper words to ourselves, attempting to define who we are.

A Biblical understanding of God's word deviates from human focus on the inner self. A Latin term, *extra nos,* describes the nature of God's word. It means "from the outside." There is a transcendent word that can't be found inside of you. When I can't tell the difference between my inner voice and indigestion, I need a word spoken to me, from outside of me.

The most powerful moments in my life involved a word from the outside. When a million other voices were screaming to be heard, God's word prevailed upon me. Someone came and spoke truth that I was deaf to hearing on my own. Or a friend gave an encouragement that delivered me from fear and uncertainty. God's word comes from beyond the realm of our own well-wishes and tells us who we are.

THE BIBLE

I understand Ava's resistance to Christianity. She has been hurt by the church and by Christians who nullify her sense of identity and meaning. We Christians must ask forgiveness for hurtful words and thoughtless judgement. But does the failure of Christians negate the Christian message? We have to examine what Christianity *really* has to say.

The Bible consists of 66 books (39 Old Testament, 27 New Testament) ranging from narrative history to poetry, prophesy to letters, wisdom to apocalyptic literature. **The message throughout is that of a loving God who pursues a lost humanity.** The words "loved" and "sent" are themes throughout, as God seeks these rebel people and chooses to redeem them.

For Christians, the Bible is authoritative. It is the bearer, in human language, of God's powerful and creative word (Rom. 10:14–17; I Cor.

2:4–5). It is a very *human text,* penned by the hands of men. It is full of emotion, rhetoric, and creativity. It was written within particular historical contexts.

At the same time, the Bible is a very *divine text.* It is God's method of operation to use people, to work *in* and *through* them. The Bible is no different. Though it is scribed by human beings, it reflects divine origin. God is the ultimate author. Why do we believe this? First, the Bible makes this claim about itself (II Tim. 3:16). Furthermore, it's helpful to see how the early church came to see these texts as inspired by God.

The early Christians quickly acknowledged what was authoritative and what was not. There was great deliberation over which texts should be included in the canon (the final collection of writings that make up the Bible). Questions and controversy served to sharpen the discernment of the early Christian church. They took seriously the task of answering, "What is truly God's word?"

As those living in the midst of the movement, the first generation of Christians were able to distinguish what aligned with Jesus' life and teaching. As those who lived within the memory of Jesus' message and ministry, they held each testimony to a high standard of truth and accuracy.

For the New Testament, one criterion for acceptance of a book or letter was that each writing must have **apostolic origins.** In other words, it must originate from one of the first disciples, personal witnesses of Jesus' ministry. The role of witness was a vital part of what it meant to be an apostle (Acts 1:22).

Another criterion for acceptance was a **consistency of message.** Though each gospel, letter, or book is unique in its own right (language, style, perspective), they have a coherent theology (Luke 24:27). It's the same God from different angles. Writings were dismissed if they deviated from the central message of the Gospel.

Our culture has doubts and questions in regard to our source. Our non-Christian friends won't share the same starting point. The Bible is often seen as outdated and irrelevant, a product of premodern people. *We know better now.* In the modern West, it's fashionable to dismiss the thoughts, beliefs, and values of people who lived millennia ago. As if somehow we are privileged to understand far more than the simple folk that lived before us.

Progress in science and reason have expanded knowledge, but not necessarily wisdom. The collective wisdom of past generations is a strong testimony to long-lasting truth. **There are some things that only prove themselves after centuries of time.** We are in danger of an arrogant and limited perspective if we dismiss enduring testimony.

Scholarly critics have dissected the Bible in sterile ways that impose post-Enlightenment Western values. No other literary text has endured such intense examination or criticism. Yet academic rigor has its limits. In the end, you will always question that which is meant to be grasped by faith. We read the Bible as we have it and for what it is, not what we wish it to be. We hear the Biblical writers out, on their own terms.

Proving the Bible is not my purpose in this book. There are solid arguments for Biblical authority. Other, more gifted individuals offer substantial reasons why we should respect the Bible's historical authenticity. My purpose here, as it would be with someone like Ava, is to *simply listen to the story the Bible tells.*

Every belief system has presuppositions. For that matter, every story asks you to accept some basic terms. Whether a movie, a book, or a story told by a grandparent, they ask you to enter their worldview. They invite you, "Come see life from my vantage point." This is what a first-century doctor named Luke expressed at the beginning of his gospel. He called it "a narrative of the things that have been accomplished among us" (Luke 1:1). He summons the reader to listen to the account of these extraordinary events.

For those who have misgivings about the Bible, I ask them to set their doubts aside for a moment. The purpose of the Bible is less about proving a point and more about telling a story. The Biblical authors were not writing to sway skeptical twenty-first century minds. They were giving an account of what God had done in their time.

A fourth-century giant of Christianity named Augustine once wrote, "Truth is like a lion. You don't have to defend it. Let it loose and it will defend itself." When talking with friends who dismiss the Bible, I simply let the truth loose. I ask them to graciously listen, without an agenda. This is the same courtesy they would ask of me, to withhold cynicism and judgement. And so I ask it of them: "Just listen. Forget everything you *think* you know about the Bible and just let the story speak for itself."

Are there things in the Bible that challenge us? Of course. There are portions of Scripture that make me squirm. This only serves to confirm its authority. A true word must challenge me. God has to say difficult things. I expect him to. If not, he's not God and the Bible is a blissful creation of my imagination. I don't want a collection of my best wishes. I want real words that both comfort and challenge me.

In the end, the Bible has stood for millennia as the authoritative foundation for millions of Christians. Through the voices of the Biblical writers, we hear a greater voice. His words prove themselves to us as we hear them and live by them. We come to accept them, not by reason alone, but by faith.

BEYOND THE PAGE

Christians believe that the word of God is more than a codified text. God is active in language beyond static ink on a page. In fact, the ink can barely contain the true substance of God's language.

The ancient texts must have an impact on present circumstances, or else they are simply a history book. More than historical data, we believe that God's Spirit animates language that brings his voice into the present tense. God is here and now. His voice is as relevant as ever. Here are some ways in which the word finds its way beyond the page.

PREACHING

In the tradition of the prophets (Is. 6:1–13) and apostles (Acts 2:14–36) a sermon is a point at which God's word is proclaimed publicly in the midst of a community. The preacher, speaking on behalf of God and from his word, formally conveys God's message (Rom. 1:16) to an assembled body of believers (I Tim. 4:13).

Boring? Often, yes. May God forgive us preachers and enhance our skills. But preaching and teaching serve to bring the transcendent word to a local time and place. A clear interpretation must be given to a particular community of people—in their language and context. This is the job of messengers and teachers.

Preaching is enhanced in Christian worship when the word enters other creative forms. In words recited together, in song and prayers, the divine word enters accessible forms. The objective word of God is applied to subjective experience. So pray for exceptional preaching and surprising worship.

CONFESSION AND FORGIVENESS

The word of God both kills and makes alive. It confronts our twisted ways and comforts wounded hearts. In this pattern, Christians are called to confess sin and then hear the declaration of forgiveness. Jesus himself has said, "If you forgive the sins of anyone, they are forgiven; if you withhold forgiveness from anyone, it is withheld" (John 20:23).

As a church, this proclamation of personal forgiveness is done publicly and privately. We may confess our sins in worship or to a single individual. And then we hear strange words in response. To our shame and guilt we hear, "You are forgiven." In a word of absolution spoken by another, you receive words of freedom. Here you don't just read it on a page. You hear it with your eardrums.

CHRIST-CENTERED RELATIONSHIPS

This is traditionally termed "the mutual conversation and consolation" of brothers and sisters in Christ. We speak and live out the word of God with one another in daily life. We are formed and strengthened by our brothers and sisters who convey God's word to us.

There is something powerful about sharing and living the word of God communally. The community of the word is a network of interdependent relationships. I call these people my family. I need them. We challenge one another. We encourage and support. We teach and learn. Guided by a common foundation, we hold each other accountable. This happens beyond one hour on a Sunday. These mutual conversations centered on the word are day-to-day.

In each of these ways, God's word proves bigger than our vocabulary. Faith in these words is more than mere intellectual assent. Sacraments, relationships, or a song sung together each convey the Gospel in their own language. God's word becomes incarnate, embedded in our experience. It is more than information. It is transformative.

HOW TO READ THE BIBLE

Biblical reading, study, and meditation are important to the Christian life. In these words, God reveals himself. Yet reading the Scriptures can be overwhelming. Although much can be said about Scriptural interpretation, the following points serve as a guide.

BIG STORY

When you're in the thick of the jungle, a map tells you where you are. With the Bible, the grand, sweeping summary of the Creed is like the 30,000-foot view. This helps us when we come down into the terrain of a particular book or verse of the Bible. No matter what part of the Bible you're in, understand that it fits within the larger narrative.

CHRISTOCENTRIC

Jesus is always the center. He is the ultimate key to the whole story of Scripture (Luke 24:26–27). Even where Christ is not explicitly mentioned, we have him in mind. Whether in the Old or New Testament, we ask, "How does Jesus fit here? How does Christ relate to this?" Even without mention of his name, we see his work—presence, pardon, and power.

SCRIPTURE INTERPRETS SCRIPTURE

Biblical texts, as diverse as they may be, are always woven within the larger body of the Bible. Scripture itself helps us understand specific texts (Acts 7). If you're struggling with one verse, examine what's around it. Compare it with similar or related verses elsewhere in the Bible (use a concordance).

SCRIPTURE IS THE CHURCH'S

Scripture is best understood, spoken, and read within the context of the community called the church (Acts 8:26–40). Reading, studying, listening, and discussing the word communally is vital. These words have always belonged to the Christian community, so listen to the word within these relationships. Don't default to the Internet. Discuss with a Christian friend, study in a small group, ask a pastor, or refer to a Biblical scholar who has devoted years of his or her life to understanding the Bible.

CONTEXT

A healthy approach to the Bible takes its context into account. What's around the text we're reading? Who wrote it, who was it written to, and under what circumstances? It helps to know *what it meant* before we ask *what it means.*

NOUNS AND VERBS

Go back to English class. The Bible is language, consisting of nouns and verbs, subjects and objects. We believe that the Bible is first about God's action, with him being the subject. So ask, "What is God doing in this particular text?" And second, "What are humans doing (or failing to do)?"

As we live with these sacred words, they change us. Whether in quiet reading or public preaching, they carry an undeniable power. By them, God reveals who he is. As we come to know him, we discover who we are.

• • •

Later in his career, Grandpa was a leader in his denomination, supervising a region of pastors. At his funeral, one of these pastors spoke. His name was Dean, and he reminisced about an odd memo Grandpa once sent. To hundreds of pastors he wrote, "Shine your shoes."

"It seemed odd," Dean remarked. "We all chuckled at his memo. But Ottmar believed that the word of God is powerful and the Gospel is of utmost importance. There must be dignity to our ministry. Shining our shoes is one way to bring this dignity to the word we declare."

This little detail was an epiphany to me. Grandpa never expressed himself as directly as I desired. Sometimes his communication was confusing. But here I saw his heart. "Shine your shoes." In his own language, he expressed his deepest conviction, his love for God's word and for people. I came to terms with the frustrating aspects of our relationship. We each have our flaws. But I'm convinced that he loved me and all his grandchildren.

I have become keenly aware of my own paternal habits. I am constantly working to be attentive to the unique needs of my children. My girls like to cuddle. The boys prefer to wrestle. For each of them, the bedtime routine consists of prayer, story, and song. And it always concludes with a kiss and the words, "Daddy loves you."

Reflect

> We often hear the popular phrase, "Listen to your heart." How is a word "from the outside" a countercultural idea?

> What would you say to a friend who believes the Bible to be "made up"?

> For much of history, a majority of the Christian church was illiterate. Some scholars say that only 10% of the population of the Roman Empire in the first century could read and write. How does God's word impact people beyond its written form?

> When have you been impacted by "a word from the outside"?

> Who is someone you know who needs to hear a word from God today? How might you be the one to deliver it?

COMMUNITY

"**G**imme the damn ball," demanded a stout boy with a fierce scowl on his face.

"I'm playin' wit it," pleaded the skinny kid.

"Boy, I be fittin' ta punch you in the mouth."

"Come on, man. I—"

Pop. Brandon dropped to the gym floor. Dozens of kids were chaotically running around. Jumping rope. Giggling. Shooting hoops. A few saw the punch and assembled for the show. I entered the cluster of children and picked up the little boy with the bloody mouth. Another adult grabbed the offender. This was my introduction to Brandon. He was eight.

I was a young pastor-in-training. Although 22 years old, I looked 17. I had come to Bethlehem Lutheran Church to gain ministry experience. As he did with all seminary students, Pastor John Schmidtke threw me in the deep end of the pool with their Wednesday night program. A hundred children walked in off the streets every week. At times it was inspiring. Most weeks it was anarchy.

I walked into the experience naively white. I learned that in this black community, a momma's wrath is worse than jail. But her love is a glimpse of heaven. I discovered an emotionally expressive culture, while I came from one that concealed feelings. I found that basketball is a means of building credibility. Like music, sport crosses lines of race and language.

Bobbi and I sang in the church gospel choir for a short stint. My attempts to sing and clap at the same time were always a half-beat behind. As awkward as I was, the people accepted me. They affirmed my effort even though I was so obviously out of place. I knew I couldn't be black, so I was just me. To this day, I'm grateful for their gracious acceptance.

My time at Bethlehem exposed me to the challenges of being black in a largely segregated city. I learned that when you watch the ten o'clock news and see another mug shot of a black male, he has a name and a story. Issues of education, economics, and politics are not black and white. They are varying degrees of gray.

From the moment I met him, Brandon taught me things I would never have known. To see them through his eyes changed me. He attended seven different schools from kindergarten through high school. Only one is open today. By failure, scandal, or consolidation, they've all shut down, evidence of a frustrated education system.

In 2011, Brandon's younger brother stole a car with some friends. Before they could ditch it, a chase ensued with the police. In a desperate attempt at escape, the 16-year-old slammed into a cop car. Now the charge wasn't just auto theft. The car was considered a weapon used against an officer. He wouldn't get out of jail until he was 20.

In August 2012, Brandon's older brother Darryl was with some friends in the wee hours of the morning. A car squealed around the corner and sprayed his vehicle with bullets. Darryl died on the scene. Brandon's arm is tattooed with his name.

I have a picture of Brandon in my office that was taken on the day he was baptized. He has his arm around Pastor Schmidtke and a goofy grin on his face. The picture reminds me that for Brandon, the church was home. An oasis. A people to cry and rejoice with.

The church, at its best, is genuine community. These are a people of honesty who know the reality of their flawed condition. These are a people of hope who believe that condition has been radically altered. Without this community, Brandon would not be where he is today.

CHURCH

The word "church" has a public relations problem. Talk to people like Ava. She'll tell you the church is boring, antiquated, hypocritical, irrelevant, greedy, and judgmental. There have been abuse scandals. Shady televangelists. Self-serving politics. Homophobic hatred. Why would anyone willingly join this association?

At this point, we must return to a true definition of the word. **Fundamentally, the church is a community gathered in and through Jesus Christ.** The early Christians used a word meaning "assembly" or "gathering" to describe themselves. The church is not a "what" or a "where," but a "who." We are *people*—often a broken, sinful, hypocritical, lying, thieving people. But we are more than just any collection of people. We are a *people called and defined by Jesus Christ.*

In the second century, church father Tertullian called the church "a hospital for sinners." It is in this "hospital" that we discover the Remedy. We are a wounded and weary people. Christ is the great Healer who binds up this tattered band. As the church, we do not claim perfection, but redemption.

Some will say that the church is purely a sociological phenomenon, a subculture of people who associate by their common interest. You can form community around anything—food, sports, art, exercise, or gaming. Though the church may include common aspects of community, its core is uncommon.

More than an affinity group, we believe this community is distinct because it is **God-inspired.** The association of Christ-followers is **a creation of God.** It is a **divine reality.** Jesus ascribed the initiative to himself: "You did not choose me, but I chose you . . ." (John 15:16). Similarly, Peter said, "Once you were not a people, but now you are the people of God" (I Pet. 2:10).

It was not our brilliant idea to worship an executed Savior. It was not our great invention to bind ourselves to a common book, a meal, or a shared standard of righteousness. Our Christian community is instigated by Christ and is animated by his Spirit.

Here it is important to note that the church is not primarily an institution. The church takes on institutional forms such as buildings, budgets, programs, and national organization. But these do not define the fundamental nature of the church. Take away denominations, steeples, and stages. Jesus will still gather his people and hold them together. Here is how the Bible describes the church:

BODY

The church is Christ's body, a communion of individuals who comprise a whole. Jesus is the head. Each person is a part. An arm, a leg, or a pinky toe. All are valued. All are unique. As diverse as the parts may be, they hold together by a transcendent unity in Christ (I Cor. 12:12–26).

BRIDE

In this metaphor, the church is the bride and Jesus is the groom. He commits himself to her. He keeps the promises he's made. He serves her, and provides for her. Although she may have blemishes and stains, he loves her nonetheless. To him she is beautiful. He loves her to the point of death, giving his own life (Eph. 5:25–32).

FOR THE WORLD

The church does not exist for itself but for the world. In surprising ways, God uses the church for his purposes on earth. The work of Jesus continues, no longer in his visible presence on earth, but by his Spirit in his followers (Acts 1:8). This humbling fact purges any self-serving motives. It confronts those who only see the church as meeting their own needs and preferences.

The church is a people who are **loved** and **sent.** We find our identity in Christ alone. His sacrificial loves defines us. It makes us a people of purpose. God is using us for his will in the world. The church is sent—to cities and towns, to hurt and need, to dark and difficult places.

SACRAMENTS

A distinctive part of being the Christ-centered community is that we devote ourselves to age-old elements. We've examined the word of God. This is certainly the fundamental foundation of our common faith. Now we turn to a mysterious and often misunderstood word: **sacrament.**

Modern life is dominated by reason and knowledge. Mankind is on a quest to tame the mystic and mysterious. Only that which is rational is believable. And so we seek answers to every question through data, money, research, and strategy. We believe that we can eventually figure out any problem, given enough time and resources.

Even so, the world is haunted by a spirit of things it can't explain. For all our knowledge and understanding, there are countless puzzles that perplex us. They can't be reduced to a tidy formula. We're left confounded by our inability to control our problems.

In his book *The Little Prince,* Antoine de Saint-Exupery wrote, "what is essential is invisible to the eye." For all of our knowledge, modern man misses what is essential. Identity and purpose can't be quantified in numbers or solved in a formula. In this context, God uses mysterious means to convey what is essential, what cannot be described by raw facts or pure data.

The word "sacrament" comes from the Latin for "mystery." Sacraments are mysterious means by which God imparts essential truth. Different Christian traditions will define and number sacraments in various ways. The definition that follows reflects my Lutheran-Christian convictions. "Sacrament" is a word the church uses to describe holy things that:

- **Christ instituted.** He commanded them.
- **Convey forgiveness and life.** They come with the promise of Christ's work in us.
- **Employ a physical element.** The word of God is joined to common material.

From my own Lutheran heritage, I recognize two events in the Bible that fit this description. One is a washing and the other is a meal. Baptism and the Lord's Supper connect us to Christ in real and mysterious ways.

It is noteworthy that sacraments use extremely ordinary elements. Water, bread, and wine are basic materials available throughout time. As such, they provide concrete sensory experiences. We can touch and taste them. This aligns with a Biblical worldview, enmeshed in creation. While many religions seek escape from the world, Christianity sits firmly in the midst of it. If God created it, he's apt to work with it. Biblical faith is physical and historical, grounded in earth, flesh, and time.

To believe in Jesus is most certainly an act of faith. After all, Jesus died and rose from death around A.D. 30. We are separated from his life and work by 2,000 years. Given this distance, there's the potential that Jesus is just another historical figure of an age long ago, not unlike Aristotle or Abraham Lincoln. In that case, our religion is merely a pious remembrance of a good man.

I am convinced that Jesus is more than a historical figure of the past. He is a person, present and active in the third millennium. One way in which he comes into present proximity with his people is through the sacraments. These mysteries are an intimate connection with the living Lord, a conduit to what he did in A.D. 30.

By words spoken, water applied, and a meal partaken, the Christian community is united with Jesus himself. In these mysterious things, we get everything he won for us on that dark Friday outside the city of Jerusalem in Palestine. His life, death, and resurrection 2,000 years past become his presence, pardon, and power for us at this very hour.

. . .

BAPTISM

Water is basic to human life. Without it, we die. With it, we live. So God chose this common element to carry the fullness of life that he gives. Water, accompanied by his word, constitutes a powerful event in the life of a Christian.

We didn't make baptism up. It has been given to us by Jesus himself (Matt. 28:19–20). Scripture uses a variety of language to describe the action that occurs in the event called baptism.

INCORPORATION

You are incorporated into the very life of Jesus, intimately united with him. An African American spiritual describes this in a refrain: "I'm wrapped up, tied up, and tangled up in Jesus." This binding union is so serious that we are joined to Jesus' journey. We die as he died. But more important, we rise as he rose (Rom. 6:3–11).

BIRTH

Like birth, baptism is life (John 3:3). As an infant is a brand-new person, so with baptism we are made new people, regardless of our chronological age. As life is given to a child, so life is given to the Christian. Just as we didn't order our own birth, so baptism is new life that is given, not taken or achieved.

WASHING

Like dirty laundry, our lives are polluted with the grease and grime of sin. So the Bible uses the language of cleansing to describe what God does in Christ through baptism (I Cor. 6:11; Eph. 5:26). The grit, dirt, and stains are removed, laundered with the Savior's blood.

MAKING DISCIPLES

Baptism inaugurates a new life as a follower of Jesus. New life means new patterns of living. The term "disciple" refers to the teaching relationship between a mentor and an apprentice. Baptism is the initiation into this lifelong relationship (Matt. 28:19–20). We are such followers of Jesus, walking close at his heels. And we invite others along our way in this pattern of discipleship.

PUTTING ON CHRIST

There is a new fashion. A new kind of style covers your body. Paul uses the language of clothing in relation to baptism (Gal. 3:26–29). You are covered with Christ, given a new identity and appearance.

Though baptism occurs once in a person's life, it marks the pattern in which our whole lives are lived: The old person is daily drowned and dies while the new person daily arises. This one-time event sets the pattern of our daily identity. It is God's name placed upon us. It is the mark of his claim. By the mysterious working of water and God's word, he says, "My child, you belong to me."

COMMUNION

In cultures around the world, meals indicate a personal intimacy between friends or family. We generally don't dine with strangers. The dinner table is for those closest to us. A feast is about more than food. It's about relationships.

A meal is central to Christian life and practice. Also known as the Eucharist ("thanksgiving") or communion ("unity" or "union"), the Lord's Supper is the meal instituted by Jesus the night before he was crucified. From that night on, communion has been just that, an intimate communion with Jesus.

Jesus' last supper is recorded in three of the four Gospels (Matt. 26:26–29; Mark 14:22–25; Luke 22:14–23). It was the celebration of the Passover, a meal repeated by the Israelites since they were freed from slavery in Egypt (Ex. 12). The meal drew upon the imagery of blood and sacrifice for forgiveness and deliverance of God's people.

Jesus built on this history and imagery by boldly inserting himself as the center of the meal. "This is my body," he claimed with broken bread in hand. "This is my blood," he declared with the wine. In doing so, he proclaimed himself the sacrifice offered for the sake of his friends. He dies so they live. He takes on the wrath so they can go free.

What does the meal mean for us today? If we take Jesus' words seriously, the meal is more than an empty ritual or sentimental reenactment of an ancient ceremony. We describe communion as **the real presence of Christ**. In a real and mysterious way, Jesus is present in the bread and wine.

"This is my body." "This is my blood." It was a somber context in which Jesus spoke these words. The mood was heavy. This wasn't the time for jokes or riddles. The context demands we take Jesus' words seriously and literally. So we believe that in an incomprehensible manner, his body and blood are present.

Jesus stated the purpose of this meal when he said that it is "poured out for many for the forgiveness of sins" (Matt. 26:28). We are at the table as an expression of our restored relationship. We are not two parties divorced by an ugly feud. The offended party (God) has forgiven the offender (us). In case we ever forget our standing with him, he welcomes us to the table. The means of reconciliation are none other than flesh and blood.

In the Lord's Supper, our communion is not only with Jesus. Our connection is also with the community. The feast is a unification with family, our brothers and sisters in Christ (I Corinthians 10:17). Though many in number and diverse in background, Jesus is our common bond. His invitation brings us to the same table.

Over the centuries, the sacraments have become sources of controversy and division. They have been subject to over-explanation and sterile doctrinal statements. And they have been reduced to ritualistic traditions, motions to go through. Amid the confusion, it's important to return to the simple center. Augustine wrote, "A sacrament is where God's love is made visible." Baptism and communion are about Jesus and his people. Here, in tangible ways, we see that we are loved.

. . .

As adults, we are asked, "What do you do?" As if our identity is found in our job or what we accomplish. But what happens when I stop working or accomplishing? Who am I then? My identity is not ultimately determined by my career or education, my finances, or accolades. Nor am I primarily defined by my ethnicity or sexuality, as if all I am is straight, white, and male.

At my core, I am defined by my relationship with the living God. All other aspects of my being flow from this fundamental reality. God says, "You are mine. You are loved." The fact that *he* says it means it is no ordinary love. Divine love is such a profound reality that it requires more than words. It is fully expressed in the language of experience, employing all the senses. His love is located in a family of people and expressed by their gathering around him.

God has rivals who wish to stake their claim on our hearts. We are attacked by distress and doubt, shame and regret. We are tempted to be who we are not. Our very identity as God's children is threatened daily.

God responds with a fierce love. I return to his grace, word, and community. With grace, he is good to us even when we don't deserve it.

With words, he declares us new people. With community, he surrounds and sustains us. "Ah, yes. I dare not forget. I am loved by God in Christ."

· · ·

Bobbi and I strolled out of the doors of Bethlehem Lutheran Church on a Sunday afternoon. Brandon was right behind us. As we approached my 1985 Oldsmobile Ninety-Eight, I saw the police car parked behind it. I had bought the Olds from my grandma two years earlier. Being Grandma's car, we called it the "G-ride." As the officer walked toward us, I saw that the back window of the car was smashed.

A 15-year-old kid named Demarco had smashed a back window, hopped in, and attempted to jack the steering column to steal the car. Where a 15-year-old learns this skill, I don't know. The officer happened to roll up on Demarco before he could start the vehicle. The boy fled and the cop chased him down. To make matters worse for the young man, he had drugs in his pocket.

"Do you want to press charges?" the officer asked. "Of course," I answered. I needed restitution, and Demarco needed consequences.

"You know him, Brandon?" I asked. "I seen him around," he replied. Brandon was only ten, but he knew who was trouble on the block.

The next time I saw Demarco was at the juvenile court. He wouldn't look at me as he read an apology. He was sentenced to community service and $500 for the window.

I felt the need to say something. I was done being angry weeks ago. With the judge's permission, I looked at Demarco and said, "I forgive you." It was silent in the small courtroom. Demarco must have thought something was wrong because he looked up. Our eyes met. It was as if he had never heard those words before.

I never saw a dollar from the kid. I regret that for two reasons. First, I never fixed the window. More important, I wonder where he is today.

Demarco was on the wrong side of the church walls that Sunday. Instead of stealing a car, what if he was sitting next to Brandon? What if this church, and not a gang, was his community? What if he was loved by these people instead of being used by thugs?

I may never know what happened to Demarco, but I've been committed to God's work through the church ever since. I believe in the mission of this community of Christ, that more people be loved and more people sent. God knows there are millions of kids like Demarco, longing for an identity and purpose.

Reflect

> What are common perceptions of the church in our culture? How does Tertullian's description of the church as a "hospital for sinners" address these misperceptions?

> How is the church as a body of believers (I Cor. 12:12–26) different than the church as a building? Or an institution?

> A sacrament is a sacred mystery. In our culture today, is that kind of language easy or hard to understand? Are people open to or turned off by talk of the mysterious?

> Baptism is a mark of our identity in Christ. Because it only occurs once in our lives, how can we be reminded of this foundational moment on a daily basis?

> A fellow Christian claims, "It's not that important to 'go to church.'" How do you respond?

THREE

WHAT IS GOD'S PURPOSE?

My 12-year-old mind was haunted by the ghost of Kathy Kinnunen. She was a year younger than me. I always sat a couple of seats behind her on the school bus. Kathy had straight black hair and teeth that hadn't quite come in straight. She possessed a boisterous energy that made her both fun loving and feisty.

The day before Christmas break, everyone boarded the bus with gifts for our teachers. Kids unveiled packages with bows, comparing their presents and hoping Mrs. Gustofson would like theirs best.

Kathy pulled a Hamburger Helper box out of her bag. I don't even remember what the gift was, only that she had "wrapped" it in the box. Like so many other times before, it was an opportunity to tear her down.

"You're so dirty," came the first voice. "Did you pull that box out of the garbage?"

"You're stupid poor," came a boy's voice. "What's wrong with you?"

"I can't believe you put it in that crappy box," attacked another voice. "You piece of trash."

She sank behind the defense of the vinyl bus seat, trying to conceal the box and her red face. The ridicule did not cease. Her excitement over the gift was now pain over her inadequacy.

On a cold Michigan morning, months later, I noticed that Kathy didn't board the bus. Word spread that her body had been found on a road not far from my house. A suspect turned into the accused. It was a young man and family friend of the Kinnunens. He had sexually assaulted her. When she wouldn't be quiet, he killed her.

By age 12, I knew the world wasn't perfect, but I had never felt the fullness of its cruelty. I had nightmares. I imagined her lifeless form, recklessly disposed in the ditch alongside that lonely gravel road.

No one talked much about it. Maybe because it was such a gruesome event in the life of this small town. Or maybe because the family lived on the margins of the social spectrum. I didn't know how to talk about it, or even whom to talk to. My mom asked me how I felt. All I could say was, "Not so good."

This moment was a cruel epiphany. I had always been a curious boy in a world of wonder, excitement, and possibility. But now everything that was good had been tainted. Beauty tarnished. Health infected. I felt a dark stain that I could not remove. I wanted to run away from my small hometown, but I sensed that no matter my destination, this darkness would follow.

The quest for identity and meaning is thrust upon us when we're confronted with death. One day someone is here. The next day, they are not. We are forced to deal with ultimate questions.

Why do such terrible things happen? What, if anything, does God do about it? When death is within reach, these questions are no longer theoretical. They are personal. You feel "not so good." This isn't a movie or a news article. Death touches *me.*

GOD'S STORY

It's difficult to trust God when you've suffered tragedy. We claim that we are loved by God in Christ and sent by him into the world. But love appears to be a fantasy and the world is wicked. Ask Ava about God's love after her father ran away with his mistress and her little sister died. Ask Becky after her sister, Kathy, was dumped in a ditch.

At some point, we all wonder what God is doing. We have to reconcile his goodness with the reality of evil in the world. In the mire of life, it's easy to lose sight of what God is up to. In the Biblical narrative, God's love is often blurry to his people. Infertility, slavery, famine, war, murder, and persecution clouded the vision of our forefathers in the faith. The people often wondered, "What is God doing?"

It takes the context of eternity to make sense of a moment. You have to see the forest to understand a few trees. Whether Old Testament Israel or the New Testament church, God's people have always returned to the big picture, God's grand story, his dominant activities. In triumph or tragedy, God's people recounted what God has always done (Ps. 75:1).

The ancient Creeds summarize the dominant activities of God: **creation, redemption, and sanctification.** The word "creed" means "I believe." The church from its earliest days crystallized the Christian faith into core statements of belief. There are three creeds common to the whole Christian church: the Apostles' Creed, the Nicene Creed, and the Athanasian Creed. Creeds encapsulate God's story in an overarching statement. They were established as a way for Christians to speak with one voice the same unchanged message generation after generation.

Here is the most concise creed, the Apostles' Creed:

I believe in God, the Father Almighty, Maker of heaven and earth.

And in Jesus Christ, His only Son, our Lord, who was conceived by the Holy Spirit, born of the virgin Mary, suffered under Pontius

Pilate, was crucified, died and was buried. He descended into
hell. The third day he rose again from the dead. He ascended into
heaven and sits at the right hand of God the Father Almighty.
From thence He will come to judge the living and the dead.

I believe in the Holy Spirit, the holy Christian Church,
the communion of saints, the forgiveness of sins, the
resurrection of the body, and the life everlasting. Amen.

In succinct fashion, the Creed provides a summary statement of the whole Bible. This has always been a simple way for Christians to answer the questions: "Who is God?" and "What is his purpose?" These words have transcended cultures, ethnicities, languages, and eras of time. Many have risked their lives to speak these statements under severe persecution and public ridicule.

We all need reorientation in the midst of trauma. Our hearts yearn to make sense of the tragic. Here the Creed concisely reminds us of God's story. It is a compass in the storm, a map in the wilderness. The Creed declares, "Here is what God has done and always will do." In all of life's madness, he still *creates, redeems,* and *sanctifies.*

We've answered, "Who is God?" in a threefold fashion: Father, Son, and Holy Spirit. Following the same structure of the Creed, let me recount what I call "God's Story." This gives us narrative context, an eternal scope to our present snippet of time.

Actions reveal intentions. Therefore this record of God's activity discloses his purpose. God's story is tragic, as it tells us that God's good and perfect creation is no longer so. But it is also a jubilant story, a declaration that he has come to win his creation back to good once again.

CREATION: GOD MAKES GOOD

O ut of selfless love, *God creates*. It's a simple but foundational truth. The world is not a series of accidents. You are not a serendipity of atoms and molecules. There is an Origin, a Source, a Maker of all things. If there is a Creator, then all things have divine focus. Every mosquito and mountain, every lily and lake, exists with intention. Every creature has purpose in a universal matrix.

The Bible employs an ordinary word to point to the nature of what God creates. It is a dominant word in the first part of Genesis: "good." (Gen. 1:4) This particular word is not used in a generic sense, as it can often take in the English language. The Hebrew word for "good" conveys *perfect intent*. It describes something that is true, right, and beautiful. Everything is in its place, and has its unique role.

"Good" means that God engineered life to hold a harmonious balance. There is astounding complexity and simplicity of the world around us. There is the *miniscule*—DNA, atoms, and molecules. And there is the *massive*—100 billion stars in the galaxy and 100 billion galaxies in the universe.

Along with "good," another mantra is recorded in the first words of the Bible: "And it was so" (Gen. 1:7, 9, 11, 15, 24, 30). This chorus underscores the reality that there is divine origin and order to everything. Each component of nature is organized. Each part fits, complementing the function of the whole. A divine design is hardwired into the DNA of every plant and animal.

"Good" is repeated after each day of Creation until it reaches a climax on the sixth day. On this day God fashioned the pinnacle of his creation, human beings created "in his image." It was then that he said, "very good." At this point, everything is the way it is supposed to be.

But every story has an antagonist. **In God's story, the irony is that creatures deny their own Creator.** Satan comes to the first humans, Adam and Eve, as a serpent. He himself rebelled against God's good order. And he tempted the two humans to do the same.

"Sin" is a religious word that's often muddled and misunderstood. Simply put, sin is **rebellion against God and his goodness.** Adam and Eve ate the fruit that the serpent gave them. It was from the one tree that God instructed them to refrain from eating from. Consuming a piece of fruit was not Adam's sin. His sin was rebelling against God's command.

Good things go bad. This is the center of our fundamental "fallenness." Sin's insidious nature is to take what's best, God's best, and spoil it. In this way, sin goes against the grain of the perfect and harmonious intent with which God created life to work. If "good" is when everything is in perfect order, then sin is chaotic disarray.

All humans are infected with this disease. Does sin mean we are *completely* bad? No, God still creates us with admirable qualities, brilliantly complex bodies, and the capacity to live life in goodness. But we are never able to attain the fullness of what God intended for us. We are saddened, frustrated, and burdened by our weakness and limitations.

In his goodness, God created us for life. The painful consequence of sin is that the goodness of life is reversed. As a result, death is the destiny of all living things. Death is the one thing every human being has in common. The "goodness" of early Genesis is now "not so good."

The masterpiece is ruined, yet God does not choose to scrap his creation and start over. Almost immediately after the fall into sin, God labored within this creation to set it right again. God's heart is revealed in his persistent desire to get his creation back. He did not abandon his shattered project. Self-giving love compelled him to recover this fractured creation. From beginning to end, Scripture is the story of this God on a mission to put things back to good again, as he created them to be in Eden.

Reflect

> Read Genesis chapters 1–3. Circle the word "good" and add up the number of times it's used.
> Many people, like Ava, have difficulty believing that God is good if life is so bad. How does the story of Creation provide a helpful response?
> Give a few examples of God's goodness in the world. Using the same examples, what happens when these good things go bad? How does this reveal sin's ability to twist what God creates "good"?
> How is the story of Creation both honest about sin and hopeful about recovery?
> How does creation show that we are loved by God?

REDEMPTION: GOD WINS BACK

A core truth in God's story is that **we are worse than we thought.** Sin holds every one of us captive. No matter how great our capacity for good, we always find ourselves enslaved to our mistakes and frailties. We are bound by ego, pride, misguided desires, regret, and shame. Not only do we suffer from our own sin, but we are also hurt by the sins of others. The undeniable proof that we are worse than we thought is the finality of death. Whether by tragedy or the slow decline of age, *everyone dies.*

If the first truth is that we are worse than we thought, the second core truth is that **God is greater than we imagine.** We often respond to the first truth by trying harder. We attempt to improve upon our self-reliance or good effort, our moral pedigree or piety. But the only real response to the first truth is for God to do something greater.

The word "redemption" describes God's great work of recovering what was lost. Redemption is commerce language. To redeem means, "to pay a price to buy something back." Its history is in the slave trade. A captive can never free himself. Someone must come and set him free. And so a slave could be purchased, redeemed out of slavery into a free life.

Redemption is a theme throughout the Biblical story. From Abraham to Moses, from kings (like David) to prophets (like Isaiah), God has always been working to restore the goodness of his world. Redemption means that God didn't scrap his creation when it was wrecked by rebellion. Instead, he chose to win it back.

The price paid was steep and surprising. To recover what was lost, God sent his Son into the fractured creation. Jesus was born with toenails and teeth, eyebrows and ears, flesh and bone. He lived a real human life, experiencing the full effect of a fallen world. Around A.D.30, the very humanity he came to save put him to death. This was the price for freeing an enslaved people. A life for a life. Blood for blood.

The Roman government executed Jesus of Nazareth as a common criminal. The cross was a Roman tool of torture and execution, common in the first century. His corpse was removed from the cross, wrapped in burial clothes, and placed in a grave.

But Jesus' death is not the end of the story. Three days later, his tomb was found empty. He was then spotted on numerous occasions over the next 40 days by more than 500 witnesses. The word for this is **resurrection**—to live again. A dead man came back to life. The cross and the grave are empty. His remains have yet to be found. At this moment, Christians believe Jesus to be the risen, mighty ruler of the entire universe.

Now resurrection is the template for all Christians. It is the reversal of the curse of sin and death. It is God's picture of what he's doing in the world—*redeeming all things back to good again.* From sin to forgiveness. From death to life. From 80 years to eternity.

With Jesus, the complete redemption of all creation has been set in motion and is advancing toward a final day of restoration. The Biblical worldview of history is linear. There is a beginning and an end to this story. So there will be a final day, known as the Last Day, the Second Coming, Judgement Day, the End.

In the end, Jesus will return, judge sin, evil, and all those who oppose him once and for all. He will usher in a new day, a new heavens, and a new earth. Jesus has come to put things back to good again, as God intended for his creation from the beginning.

Reflect

> Read Exodus 6:6–8 and Ephesians 1:7–10. How does redemption from slavery relate to redemption from sin?
> Give an example of how a particular sin traps and enslaves.
> Do you think that most people would agree or disagree with the statement, "We are worse than we thought?"
> How is Jesus' work "greater than we imagine"?
> How does redemption illustrate that we are loved by God?

SANCTIFICATION: GOD TRANSFORMS

Within the scope of God's story, we live in an "in-between time." We are in-between Jesus' first coming and second coming. It is a time of *tension*. On the one hand, things are still "not so good." On the other hand, God is actively working redemption in the world. On the one hand, hatred and fear remain as vile as ever. On the other hand, a reign of love is advancing in Jesus' name. Crosses are erected around the globe, marking God's claim on rebel territory.

This time of tension is confusing. What do we do? There are many options. Despair. Self-preservation. Bare survival. Apathy. For the Christian, God's love inspires an unlikely hope. God's redemption means that we have God-given destiny, not only eternally, but even in the time of tension.

"Sanctification" means "to make holy." Sanctification is God's work in the middle of the tension. It is the messy work of attending to a people who are "not so good," restoring them to God's good intention. Surgery is the repair of broken body parts. Sanctification is the Spirit's procedure upon broken minds and hearts.

Sanctification does not mean that we make ourselves holy, but that God does. The Holy Spirit works to transform us, day by day, into the people he intends for us to be. You are a work in progress. God isn't finished with you yet. The Holy Spirit daily forms and shapes you into the person God has always intended for you to be. Some days are a leap forward. Other days we take two steps back. Yet the Spirit is persistent, working *on* us and *in* us.

A surprising facet of God's story is that he also works *through* us. God employs people for his work in the world. He gives them a vital role in his universal plan of redemption. He transforms us for really important work—that we might actively participate in his transformation of others. Christians are not passive, lazy, or resigned to indifference. The Spirit compels and conforms us for God's holy work.

We are given the name "church," a people gathered in Jesus Christ. Not a building, place, or institution. We are a ragged band of pilgrims journeying through this time of tension.

Imperfect and ordinary as we are, sanctification means we are meant for more. God's power in the world is made evident through the frailty of his followers. Possessed by the Holy Spirit and animated by his power, we do the mission God has placed before us.

Jesus gave his people clear purpose in the world. We find this in the **Great Commandment** (Matt. 22:37–39) and the **Great Commission** (Matt. 28:19). The Great Commandment calls us to love God and love our neighbor (anyone around us) as ourselves. The Holy Spirit transforms us for this work, enabling us to worship God and live as remarkable neighbors in the world.

The Great Commission is Jesus' imperative to "Go and make disciples of all nations." His mission is expansive. His word must multiply. God's work of redemption in Jesus is global, trans-historical, and cross-cultural. The message of Jesus is always spreading throughout the world through his people.

Sanctification is an adversary of self-righteousness. There is no room for arrogance or overconfidence. Sanctification is God's activity, not our own heroic effort. In humility, we give him the credit for our transformative makeover. Only he could transform darkness into light, cold into warmth, fear into love.

By God's inspiration, we love our cities, care for our neighbors, serve the poor, and passionately give witness to God's plan for the world. We never know when the End may come. Jesus may return ages from now . . . or tomorrow may be the Last Day. Until that day, we labor on in this time of tension. We work with serious urgency and profound purpose. We have God's work to do. We endure discomfort, hardship, and suffering because we have hope in a new day, "the resurrection of the dead and the life everlasting."

• • •

What is God's purpose? The heart of the Christian message is that God loves a lost humanity. What he created "good" is fractured. It's "not so good." But he still wants us, even though we fail to acknowledge him. In sending Christ, he wins us *back to good again.*

As an adult I made contact with Kathy's sister, Becky. She still lived in the small town we grew up in. I always wanted to talk to her about Kathy's murder, but in my youth I didn't know how.

I wanted Becky to know the pain that I felt at Kathy's death. I wanted her to know she was not alone, that we don't gloss over the gnarly, twisted horrors of life. And I wanted her to know I was sorry. As a boy, I was unable to show her compassion or offer help.

When Becky responded, I expected to hear grief and even bitterness. Her response surprised me. She said, "I did a lot of praying when I was a kid, and I don't remember what I was praying for. But I remember telling myself that I forgive the man who took my sister's life."

Kathy's murderer is in prison for life. Becky told me that his own family cannot forgive him. They say he doesn't deserve it. I don't remember Becky as being "religious" or "churchgoing." Nonetheless, God radically impacted her story, even in tragedy.

When all we see is tragedy, it's easy to lose hope. It seems impossible for life to ever be "good again." Yet Becky speaks of another reality. She ended her letter, "For me, yes, there has been healing. I believe it's because I asked God for his strength to help me, and he's given it to me and I know he always will."

Becky doesn't attempt to answer the "why" of her sister's death. For her, that's the wrong question. Rather than ask "why," she has faith in *who* God is and *what* he is ultimately doing. She believes that God creates, redeems, and sanctifies. So she trusts him for *who he is,* even when she doesn't know *why* things happen.

Reflect

> A Christian says, "I'm saved. I don't have to do anything except wait for heaven." What would you say in response?
> The "time of tension" is the time between Christ's first and second coming. Give two or three examples of this tension, where you see both "good" and "not so good" at the same time.
> What do you say to someone who thinks all Christians are self-righteous? How does an understanding of sanctification assist your response?
> God's story has an end that could come at any moment. How does this affect our everyday life?

FOUR

WHAT IS MY PURPOSE?

The devil is loudest at night, between 1:00 and 4:00 a.m. It was the early years of parenting. As a husband, I was a work in progress. Add a new career, homeownership, and a screaming infant. I was a novice in trades I had never practiced before.

Our second child, Joshua, screamed for months through successive ear infections. This was accompanied by projectile vomiting. Pain awakened him at 2:00 a.m. I stumbled up the narrow stairs to the nursery, angry with him for waking me up. My wife and I were both zombies.

When I lifted his sweaty body from the crib, my anger became guilt for feeling frustrated with a baby. I called him "Mancub" from Rudyard Kipling's *The Jungle Book*. Like the character Mowgli, Joshua was "the man's cub." I placed his head on my shoulder, attempting to soothe his pain.

A screaming baby contributed to my insomnia. I hadn't slept more than three hours a night for months. I was too awake to be tired and too tired to be awake. Even when everyone else was sleeping, I lay awake, my mind recycling thoughts of doubt and fear.

Every fear is magnified by darkness. A refrain of thoughts replayed in my head: "I'm a failure. I'm so ineffective. What a mess-up." After a few months, I started drinking a little before bed. For the first time, I understood addiction's allure. The self-medication of drugs, alcohol, or food can dull the distractions. I thought a little sip would temper the devil's voice in the night. Instead, it only amplified his words.

His most haunting whisper is, "You don't matter." What if the world never noticed my absence? The thought of having no purpose is a fatal one. In daylight, the devil's words appear irrational, but at night . . . they materialize into something believable.

Satan bit in that dark nursery, stinging me somewhere between the crib and rocking chair. *What if this was all done? What if you drove the car off the overpass? "It was a tragedy," they would say. "A young man, so much life ahead of him," they would say.* It was a seed of thought that terrified me with its appeal. I whispered in the dark, "I don't matter."

The following night, another scream at 1:00 a.m. It pierced my ears and my gut. *She'll get him,* I thought. But I knew my wife would be up early to feed him in a few hours. "I'm awake, I may as well." I trudged up the stairs muttering, "Another night of hell."

The boy lay sweaty, hair matted with vomit. I stumbled around the room, cleaning the wailing child and his crib. A voice echoed off the walls: "You're a shitty father. Your kid is crying and you're pissed about it. Do you hate your own son? How could you?"

I was shaking. I tasted the salt of the sweat dripping down my forehead. "I'm not right," I kept repeating. A cocktail of anxiety and adrenaline pulsated through the veins in my neck. *You don't matter!* The whisper grew to a wail.

Then sudden silence. It was jarring. Joshua's crying ceased. The voice was gone. I felt like a zombie that had returned to humanity. I emerged from a daze. *What's wrong? Where am I? Did something happen? Is the baby okay?*

I looked down to see his head cradled in the crook of my elbow. His blue eyes turned slate in the moonlight through the window. He had babbled incoherently for weeks, but now he uttered something that shocked me: "Da." My son called my name.

In that moment a new voice entered my inner ear: "Call me. Call me Father." My sweat was replaced with tears. I could not contain them. The boy's soft fingers encircled my thumb and squeezed. The Lord's Prayer begins with this call: "Father." And I have prayed that prayer with each of my children at bedtime ever since.

The devil is loudest between 1:00 and 4:00 a.m., but God brings the dawn. *Do I matter? Do I have purpose? What am I supposed to do?* We long to be useful, to be of some value to those around us.

The Scriptures insist on the urgency of God-given purpose. There is important work to do in the world—here, now. And God invites us into the adventure of fulfilling these vital tasks. Christianity is not simply a path to heaven. It is an unobstructed focus on the love of God in Christ. When Christ is central, every day's moment is full of meaning.

The call of Christ imprints a claim upon us: "You are loved. Do you doubt that? Look to my cross." Consequently, **those who are loved by Christ are sent by him.** We are needed. In his hands, we are not only useful, but also essential.

"You have something important to do. If you don't do it, it won't get done." Every Christian has a mission that he or she is meant to accept. The greater the burden of need around us, the greater the expectation that we are necessary for meeting that need. Love unleashes us for present responsibilities. This is the dynamic motion of *loved* and *sent*. **You matter to God, and he makes you matter to others.**

LOVE

Rizzo made a bold prediction about me. And it came true. I was walking across the parking lot when she said to a friend, "I'm going to marry that guy." We had yet to meet.

I was a 20-year-old college student dating my high school sweetheart. After my sophomore year, I signed up to be a summer camp counselor at Camp Luther in Three Lakes, Wisconsin. It was a three-month adventure among the endless lakes and pine trees of the Northwoods of Wisconsin.

Her camp name was Rizzo. Bobbi was a feisty Wisconsin farm girl known for her tight curly hair and witty sarcasm. For the first half of the summer, she wanted nothing to do with me. Other than a couple of sharp remarks, she rarely addressed me personally. I was both intrigued and confused by this girl.

In early July I discovered a new piece of information. It was swim time. The cool water of Range Line Lake awaited us, along with a hundred screaming campers. I was changing in a small dorm room with three other male counselors when Mark said, "You know Rizzo likes you, right?"

Attempting to change in a space far too small for four men, I nearly missed his comment. I muttered, "Huh?" In the rush of swim time, my three roommates stumbled out the door and into the chaotic crowd rushing to the lake. "I like her, but I thought she hated me," I confessed to an empty room.

From that moment on we began talking. A lot. Cordial conversation led to late-night forums on family, dreams, and the future. With campers fast asleep, we sat by the crackling fire till the wee hours. I was so interested in this girl. *Who is she?* I had discovered no human being like her in my 20 years. I thought of her as a tootsie pop—rock-hard on the surface but tender at the heart.

With the camp season nearly over, we spent every spare moment figuring out who the other was. One night, we sat under the starry canopy on the athletic field. The grass was cool and wet with dew. Pine trees sharply scented the evening air. "My brother has ADHD," she said. "He's a real spaz. But I love him." My response was interrupted by the sound of snorting and grunting.

Something lumbered through the dark shadows of the forest 50 yards away. The pace quickened to a gallop as paws pounded the ground below. The bear circled our position for 15 tense minutes. When we were certain it was clear, we sought the protection of a fortress.

With no flashlight we blindly followed a trail to Ark Village, nestled deep in the woods. Inspired by Noah, the ark was a fortress of lumber in the shape of a large ship. Campers slept in hammocks mounted in the hull. We finally saw the dim light of a waning campfire outside the ark.

With campers and counselors asleep, we caught our breath in the glow of the dying fire. I turned to look into her eyes. They were wide with expectancy. She was unlike any woman I had met. We were so much alike and yet so different.

I leaned toward her silhouette. As my lips neared hers, I whispered, "This is going to change everything." Before the kiss, she replied, "It already has."

I know, it sounds like the tender ending of a romantic comedy. But it happened. Her blind prediction was right. (She's almost always right.) We got married two years later. At the time I thought I loved her more than I could ever love someone. In fact, I worried that my feelings for her were unsustainable. I feared that our love would flame out as fast as it ignited.

At 20 years old, my knowledge of love was in its infancy. With time, the romance and infatuation subsided. Only then would I discover the enduring depth of love.

THE GREATEST COMMAND

Ava's impression of Christians was that they wanted to impose their beliefs on others. It seemed that their sole purpose was to make everyone just like them. Jacob seemed different. He held deep convictions but seemed genuinely interested in those who didn't share those convictions. Rather than conquer, his motive was to care.

What are we supposed to do with our lives? How do you live a life that matters most? Jesus answered questions of purpose in concise statements called **The Great Commandment** and **The Great Commission.** Here, I'll take up the Great Commandment, which hinges on the word "love."

In a stunning and simple sentence, Jesus gives clarity to life's aim. "Love the Lord your God with all your heart and with all your soul and with all your mind . . . and love your neighbor as yourself" (Matt. 22:37–39; Deut. 6:5). Single or married, child or adult, rich or poor, black or white, this transcendent responsibility has universal application. We are sent to give the love we first received from God.

On the surface, the Great Commandment may seem to be a harmless truism. There are a million memes, posters, and slogans that turn love into a cliché. "All you need is love." "Love conquers all." "One love." "Love wins."

Don't let the Great Commandment fool you. It is not another bumper sticker. Behind the kindly exterior is a forceful declaration. Jesus revealed the intensity of the command when he said, "Greater love has no one than this, to lay down one's life for one's friends" (John 15:13). Elsewhere, he went even further and called his followers to "love your enemies" (Matt. 5:44).

Jesus' Great Commandment to "love your neighbor as yourself" exposes the selfless nature of love. A "neighbor" is defined as anyone around you. We don't get to choose who is, *or who is not,* our neighbor. In Jesus' parable of the Good Samaritan, the Samaritan traveler's proximity to the roadside victim made him a neighbor (Luke 10:25–37). This proximity to another human being in need trumped any ethnic, religious, and political barriers.

The gay activist and conservative evangelical preacher are neighbors. The NRA lobbyist and the vegan tree-hugger are neighbors. The Kansas wheat farmer and the Syrian refugee are neighbors. The Great Commandment makes no requirement of worthiness. Is someone next to you? That's your neighbor.

The boundaries of love are stretched further when we notice Jesus' special concern for the most vulnerable. He elevated the worth of the lost and lowly. He healed the outcast leper and demon-possessed. He was attentive to children and women, of particular significance in first-century society. He prized the poor and marginalized "sinners, tax collectors, and prostitutes."

At a second glance, love is harder than we anticipated. Functioning on two hours of sleep with a newborn. Giving money away instead of spending it. Working extra hours to relieve someone else's load. Walking the long road of sobriety with a friend. Choosing a less lucrative career in order to impact more people. Giving up a beloved hobby to give more time to people. Forgiving someone who hates you. Meeting the needs of the poor in substantive ways. Seeking to understand someone whose lifestyle is extremely different than your own.

There is a problem with actually doing this kind of love. *That problem is us.* We are plagued by a preoccupation with ourselves. I am challenged to overcome my pride and preferences for the sake of others. I like control and comfort. Fear is a persistent reality, and I find myself acting out of self-preservation more than selfless love.

Christians are not immune to the magnetism of self. We often talk about how evil the world is while we stumble over our own self-interest. Maybe this is why those outside of Christianity accuse Jesus' followers of hypocrisy—because it's true!

We're too experienced in our failures to ever say we're perfect. We're well practiced in our sins. We recognize the reality that while we are loved by God and redeemed from our selfishness, it is not yet eradicated. We live in the painful tension of being a sinner and saint at the same time.

Jesus' call to this selfless love is *not* attainable without a superhuman capacity. Therefore the only way to love like him is to first *be* **loved.** In other words, the passive precedes the active. **Only those who *are* loved are capable of loving.**

To submit to the cross of Christ is to succumb to this love and be possessed by it. Those who are loved by God are called to love like him. Inspired by cross-born love, only then are you capable of enduring pain, scorn, humiliation, and injustice for the sake of others. By the peculiar way of the cross, love empowers us to extend its reach.

Our inability is not an excuse to avoid the command. The task set before us is too important to dismiss. To increase the seriousness of the mission, we notice that loving God and loving others are tied together. "Love the Lord your God . . . and your neighbor as yourself." The twofold command is merged into one by a hinge.

To love God is to love others, and to love others is to love God. We dare not discount anyone as beyond the scope of love, no matter how wicked. By denying them love, we deny love for God. Where else would he have us show him devotion and commitment? Is there a better way to honor him than to extend to others the love he first gave to us?

In the end, the Bible speaks of God's love as a verb. It acts. It does. It takes initiative. It gives. "God so loved the world . . ." (John 3:16). And those who are loved also love in turn. "My command is this: Love each other as I have loved you" (John 15:12). No more questions. No more doctrinal debates. No more pious church talk. Just go and love as you have been loved.

HABITS OF LOVE

The Great Commandment is strenuous to live out. Yet we do not abandon the call. We confront the challenge head on by taking the command seriously. We bind ourselves to a high standard. Cross-born love is ambitious, and often painful, but it's worth it. The lure of love is that we have already been loved in this way. Here are some tangible ways to live out the selfless love defined by Jesus. You might call them *habits of love*.

PRESENCE

An elementary component of "loving your neighbor" is proximity. To love others, we must be **present** with them. There's no time to be stuck behind the screen of a TV or phone. We can't remain tucked within the safe boundaries of our house. We dare not linger in places that keep us distant from the needs of others. Love harkens us to the active spaces of life. Homes, yards, parks, streets, and sidewalks. Stores, schools, cafés, and YMCAs.

It is vital to be present not only in a space, but also in time. Too often we are physically near someone but practically absent. We find ourselves engrossed in silence or social media. We are distracted by worry, multitasking, tomorrow's to-do list, and overcrowded calendars. How can we be present in a moment? Love means that when we are with someone else, he or she is the most important person at that moment.

Present also means that we love people as they are, not as we wish them to be. We love them in their present state, with all their warts, blemishes, and bad habits. We acknowledge that none of us is as we should be. If God is not repulsed by our rough edges, we refuse to walk away from people in their darkest moments. Love remains present.

LISTENING

To love your neighbor means *you have to know your neighbor*. Even more, to "love your neighbor as yourself" means that you have to know your neighbor *as well as you know yourself*. This is to say that the Great Commandment requires you to **listen.**

We can learn a bit of wisdom from the medical profession. A doctor says, "Listen to your patients. They'll tell you the answer." What does a doctor do when you come in for a visit? Does he prescribe a remedy as soon as you walk through the door? No, a competent physician asks, "What hurts? When does it hurt? What brought it on? How long has this been going on?" By listening to the patient, the doctor diagnoses the problem.

Too often, Christians give answers to questions people aren't asking. It's like administering chemo when the problem is a broken foot. We speak too quickly and listen too slowly. Listening requires us to shut our mouths and open our ears.

I must ask questions that get at the ultimate question of, **"Who are you?"** And then I need to shut up long enough to hear the answer. Before you can know what to say or how to help, you have to know who you're speaking with. Ask questions like:

Where are you from? What was it like growing up?
What's the hardest thing you've ever done?
Tell me the story behind your tattoo.
Tell me about your family.
What gives you the greatest sense of fulfillment?

SACRIFICE

I discovered the sacrificial nature of love as a 20-year-old summer camp counselor. A few hours of sleep on a cot or short mattress. Eating last and fast. Cleaning up puke. Giving all my energy to a new group of kids every week. Counseling a 13-year-old living with the pain of divorce. Dealing with a child's depression, ADD, or anger issues. It became clear: *This is not about me.*

Sacrifice means to give something up for someone else. The most extreme form of sacrifice is to give up your very life. Sacrifice is love's logical outcome. If you genuinely love someone, you *will* sacrifice for him or her. Love isn't love until it gives something up.

Sacrifice is counterintuitive in a status-seeking society. We are conditioned to hold on to things rather than give them up. We strive after bigger and better. More prestige, honor, admiration, and influence. To sacrifice these pursuits is considered foolishness. It is incredibly challenging to release the most valued possessions and people in our lives. We clench the things we love with white knuckles.

Jesus himself is the paragon for this counterintuitive notion. He said, "For even the Son of Man did not come to be served, but to serve, and to give his life as a ransom for many." (Mark 10:45). Although his status is rightly that of the world's King, he chose the lowest status. He became a slave in order to free the enslaved. He gave up all that was his. His dignity and rights were cast aside.

An old Latin phrase, *servire est regnare,* means "to serve is to reign." It is strange that the highest position in God's kingdom . . . *is the one with the lowest status.* The greatest office . . . *is that of a servant.* This is an unlikely truth in our world. You will spend a lifetime attempting to understand it.

I remember a college professor lecturing a class of highly motivated, highly successful undergrads. Soon this class would be in society, finding jobs with endless upward mobility. He addressed them saying, "As you prepare for your professional career, know this. We need our best to go to the places of greatest need. **Strength is for service, not status.**" Sacrifice is not concerned with status. It is love proven in service to others.

RISK

C.S. Lewis said, "Only a real risk tests the reality of a belief." Do we really trust God? Do we believe that he has loved us and sent us? Do we trust him to go with us as we extend his reign of love into the world? Only a real risk will test our belief.

Most of us are risk averse. We prefer conservative investments. We prefer the predictability of routine. We tend to the safety of what we know versus the uncertainty of what we don't.

The Bible is not a story of safety; it's a story of risk. To create the world, God risked the possibility that it could be corrupted. To make a covenant—a binding promise with his people—he risked that it could be violated. The whole story is about a messy people and a God who risks everything to win them back. With a bloody cross, we see that God risked at great expense. Good Friday proves his broken humanity was worth the risk.

Selflessly loving your neighbor puts you at risk. It leaves you vulnerable. Every time you give something, you risk losing it or getting hurt. A hug can be denied. A helping hand can be resented. A word of encouragement can fall on deaf ears. Sometimes your most heroic effort can be reciprocated with hatred. But love is not deterred by hostility. It still takes the risk.

PRAYER

As we live the Great Commandment, we are assaulted with decisions, dilemmas, headaches, and crises. Love is hard. We quickly find that it requires more than we can give. A neighbor's cancer is unaffected by treatment. A feud between family members escalates. The city's crime rate spikes.

Love leads us to pray. Because we live in the world and not a monastery, we pray with our eyes wide open. There is no room for polite prayers spoken out of pious obligation. We see the need before us and run to God with a pleading cry.

It is of fundamental importance that Jesus begins the Lord's Prayer with the address, "Father" (Matt. 6:9). **Jesus teaches prayer not as a "how to" but a *Who*.** We don't believe in the power of prayer, but in the power of the one we pray to. Jesus directs us beyond a formula. Prayer is more than what we pray. It's about the *Who* we pray to. By inviting us to call on him as Father, this prayer is an expression of a relationship.

The Great Commandment and the Lord's Prayer are parallel in their order. The Great Commandment calls us first to love God with all our "heart, soul, mind, and strength." So the first three petitions of the Lord's Prayer are oriented in this direction. We seek his name to be hallowed above all. We ask for his kingdom activity to come among us. We submit to his will, asking for it to be done on earth as it is in heaven. Thus, both the command and the prayer are first aligned with God's position, submissive to his leadership.

Then the Great Commandment pivots from love of God to "Love your neighbor as yourself." So too, the Lord's Prayer turns to our own needs and those of our neighbors. We pray for "daily bread." This means anything we need to sustain our lives. "Daily bread" includes health, safety, food, shelter, good families, good government, good education, a good economy, and the list goes on.

Next we pray for forgiveness, God's forgiveness for us and our forgiveness for others. "Forgive us our trespasses as we forgive those who trespass against us." We are asking God to restore the damage done within relationships where love has been compromised.

Finally, we pray deliverance from "temptation" and "evil," that God would strengthen us in our resolve to follow him and his ways. As we love God and love our neighbor, we expect resistance. Our prayer is for the Father's leadership in the face of harm, calamity, and the assault of the evil foe.

In this way, the Lord's Prayer guides us in a pattern of love for God and for neighbor. Love longs to pray for those it seeks. So Christians pray early and often (I Thess. 5:17). We approach the Father with all our needs (Matt. 6:9; Ps. 102:1).

The prayer born out of love for God and love for neighbor is a bold prayer. It is not timid or tame. Jesus once described a persistent widow as a picture for how to pray (Luke 18:1–8). The widow was audacious, tenacious, and relentless in asking for justice. Like this widow, he calls us to persistent dialogue. We are to "ask, seek, and knock," to plead, pull, and pester him. In doing so, we express the Great Commandment.

. . .

I married the girl. We were blind to all that marriage meant, but that's okay. We have to start somewhere. Love does not seek instant success. Instead, it is practiced through persistence and patience over the course of decades.

Three years into our marriage, we were expecting our first child. With giddy joy we went to the doctor's office. I remember staring at the ultrasound monitor in emotional shock. There was no movement on the screen, no sign of a beating heart. The ultrasound tech grew somber. "I'm so sorry, honey," she said to Bobbi. I didn't notice my bride weeping until the tech left to get the doctor.

The next few days were sadness in the extreme. There was a surgery for Bobbi. There was the sorrow relived every time someone asked about our baby. There was the hurt of losing a hoped-for child. It's hard to describe what it's like to miss someone you've known but never met.

Through this valley, our marriage could have sustained serious damage. It's one thing to love someone in the carefree happy days. It's another to love in a season of grief and suffering. For that matter, it's easy to "love God" when life falls into perfect place. Wait until everything rips apart at the seams. This is where the Great Commandment leads us. In the shadow of the cross, we love through pain and suffering. Trial is love's proving ground.

Reflect

> What distinguishes the Great Commandment from other "love slogans"?

> When is your love for your neighbor most tested? In other words, when is it hardest to love?

> Which of the habits of love—presence, listening, sacrifice, risk, prayer—do you find most intriguing? Are there other "habits of love" that you would add?

> What do you think of the statement, "Only those who *are* loved are capable of loving"?

> Consider the name or names of people you feel God has sent you to love. Apply these questions to their situation.

  • **Presence:** Where is your neighbor, and are you willing to meet that person where he or she is?

  • **Listen:** What are the greatest needs your neighbor has?

  • **Sacrifice:** What will you give up for this person?

  • **Risk:** What risks do you take in loving your neighbor?

  • **Prayer:** What needs are you praying for in regard to your neighbor?

CALLING

His broccoli cheddar soup was steaming, but Brandon wasn't eating. The restaurant bustled with customers. Brandon stared blankly at a toddler plastering her face with macaroni and cheese. His soup was getting cold. Something was wrong.

Now 23 years old, Brandon had defied all expectations. I admit that I doubted. I was at his high school graduation. He had worked so hard for that diploma. I bear-hugged him. His green graduation gown was damp with tears. He wept for an hour after the ceremony, hugging every classmate. I thought this was the pinnacle of his education. Now he would find a job.

Instead, Brandon was the first in his family to enroll in postsecondary education. It's always hardest for the pioneer. Add to that a learning disability, a stutter, and limited resources. I didn't think he could manage the rigor of college. I wanted to hold his hand, almost force him through the process. But he had to do this on his own.

I regret the doubts I had. The man sitting across from me was attending a community college. He had a job. He had his own apartment. He had come so far, pleasantly surprising us all. But on this day, he wasn't himself.

He finally broke his silence. "When I was little, I used to hit myself to get the word out."

"What?" I asked.

"You know, my stutter."

"Oh, yeah."

"Like, I'd hit my chest or my shoulder. It helped me get the word out."

"I never knew that."

"I was embarrassed by it when I was a kid. I was afraid of school 'cause I thought I would fail . . . I didn't want to fail." Tears collected in his eyes, not quite dropping to his cheek.

"Why are you telling me this?" I inquired.

"You know that planner you gave me at the beginning of the school year?"

"Yeah." I vaguely remembered it.

"I left it on the bus and now it's gone. I'm sorry. I didn't want to tell you. I don't want to fail."

"Brandon, it's okay. We'll get you another."

"And now I've been off my schedule. And my grades aren't good. And I can't focus. I didn't want to tell you. I don't wanna let you and Bobbi down."

"Brandon, you can't let us down. You know we love you."

"I know. But I'm not sure I can make it. It's hard."

"Of course it's hard."

"My family don't know. Nobody done college before. They don't know how hard it is."

"I do. I know."

I realized that Brandon was stuck in the trees. He needed to see the forest. His present struggles necessitated a broader context. He was desperate for a reason, a calling.

• • •

What's my calling in life? What's my purpose? What should I do next? Which direction should I take? These questions are asked by a 15-year-old trying to find herself in high school. They are pondered by a 23-year-old stumped about what to do after college. And a 47-year-old in a midlife crisis. And a 70-year-old who feels useless in retirement. The need for purpose and direction in life is a universal human need. **What's your calling?**

The word "sent" carries with it an urgent sense of calling. It implies that there is a place and a people who need you. You are deployed for important, God-given tasks. Your time, presence, and skills are necessary, and so you are sent to make use of them.

Many of us lack a compelling purpose. For a number of reasons, we live in an age of discontent. Some of us have a track record of mess-ups and failures. Others suffer from self-doubt and low self-esteem. Many feel inadequate. Boredom forces us to ask, "Is this it?" We wonder if there is greener grass on the other side.

In this age of discontent, we hear, "Do what you want to do. Do what makes you happy." Still, countless people are let down by unfulfilled desires. They pursue happiness but are never happy. There's a difference between what you *want* to do and what you're *called* to do. The answer to "What is your calling?" runs deeper than happiness.

VOCATION

The word "vocation" gives the Christian an unmistakable reason to live. It comes from the Latin *vocatio,* which means "to call." Calling is about more than just your job or what you do for a living. It includes all of the God-given responsibilities placed upon you.

There are four general realms that each Christian lives in. These spheres are common to each of us. Yet within them, our particular vocations are as unique as a fingerprint. Consider your unique imprint in each of the four realms.

HOME

You are called to be a brother or sister, father or mother, son or daughter, niece or nephew, and so on. Within the common elements of family, my specific niche is unique. Though there are many husbands in the world, I am the *only* husband to my wife Bobbi. Though there are many brothers in the world, I am the only brother to Anne and John.

OCCUPATION

A teacher imparts knowledge to children. An IT specialist contributes to a system that makes a whole company run efficiently. A garbage man maintains a sanitary city. You are a classmate or coworker. You have a unique skillset and capacity that you exercise in a profession or job.

Though a job certainly provides income to live on, it also bestows a deep sense of fulfillment and satisfaction. Your occupation isn't only about you. It functions for others (see the Great Commandment). Scripture is clear that we are given meaningful work to do here on earth (Gen. 2:18; Rom. 12:1). Our work is good for the planet, society, friends, and neighbors.

SOCIETY

You are a next-door neighbor, a voter, a taxpayer. You are customer or client within a functioning economy. You are a volunteer, a block captain, a friendly smile on the sidewalk or in the store. Our general place as citizens in a wider society is important. Collectively, we work for peace, justice, and prosperity in our communities, cities, states, and country.

CONGREGATION

You are a fellow worshiper, an elder, a committee member. You are a singer, a teacher, an encourager. You are a brother or sister in Christ to a local community of Christians.

Like a snowflake, each of us has a one-of-a-kind design. My particular portfolio of vocations is distinct from anyone else's. Here are some characteristics of vocations that give us a sense of meaning and purpose:

GOD-GIVEN

I once searched for baby names on the Internet. I came across some extraordinarily uncommon ones like "Awesome," "Handsome," and "Boss." As I was thinking about Awesome as a 15-year-old freshman in high school, I was reminded that names are *given*. You did not choose your name.

In a similar way, a calling is like a name. It is given to you. Like the words "loved" and "sent," the word "called" is passive. If you are called, someone else is doing the action and taking the initiative. Though we play a role in discerning our vocations, we believe that ultimately our callings are **God-given.**

This is an offensive concept in our individualistic society. A sacred value for Americans is freedom of choice. We hear this value in statements like "Follow your dreams," "Do what you want as long as you're happy," "Let your heart be your guide," and "Don't let anyone tell you what to do."

A Biblical concept of calling challenges the dreams of our hearts. God gives us reason and the ability to discern, but a deeper calling trumps our best ideas and desires. Our feelings, passions, and emotions are involved, but a greater force overwhelms the whim of our wishes.

A Biblical understanding of vocation insists that God is working in and through us. We are agents of God's will and work in the world. Our lives serve as a means for God to dispense his love and care to those around us. A farmer tills the soil because God desires to provide food for the man's community. A foster parent tucks an orphan into bed because God wills for the child to have a home. Our deepest callings are divinely originated.

The meaning of vocation is not only pragmatic. There is a more profound urge within our callings. For a Christian, vocations are holy. They are holy because God has called us to them. In our vocations, we believe that God is at work *through* us. He whispers in our ear, "You are vital. You are necessary." Our unique skills and experiences make us a valuable commodity for our family, neighbors, community, and country.

FOR OTHERS

These holy callings serve the purpose of impacting others. Paul wrote, "For you were called to freedom, brothers. Only do not use your freedom as an opportunity for the flesh, but through love serve one another" (Gal. 5:13). In this sense, mundane and boring tasks take on divine significance.

We typically see work as a means to make money. Within the realm of God-given calling, the purpose is firmly focused on others. Cleaning the house becomes a necessary and God-pleasing task that blesses others. A series of files composed in a cubicle impact a company that provides goods and services to the public. Vocation is about more than just profit. It's about people.

The reality that others need us fills our vocations with urgency and humility. With urgency—our service is needed *now*. The necessity of our work is imminent. This drives us to great humility. My callings are not about personal ambition, gain, or pleasure. My career, family, or position is for someone else. There is no room for arrogance, apathy, or hoarding.

Within the context of covenant, God said to Abram, "I will bless you and make your name great, so that you will be a blessing" (Gen. 12:2). The words "so that" are significant. They express an intended result. God blessed Abram *so that* he would be a blessing. His call was bigger than his own happiness or pleasure. **It was for others.**

God's intention for your callings is not to make all your dreams come true. That's Disney's goal. His intention for your vocations is to bless others. Your own blessings are not to be selfishly hoarded. There is purpose in your blessing.

Have you been given wealth? Share it. Have you been given a great family? Adopt others into it. Have you been called to a position of influence? Use it for the sake of others. God-given vocations are always for the good of your neighbor. Our callings are the place for us to live out the Great Commandment, loving our neighbor as ourselves.

SIGNIFICANCE

My wife and I once calculated how many diapers we had changed. We estimated that four kids over 10 years came out to 26,000. There was some discrepancy over who changed the majority of those diapers. I initially said 60/40 me. She said 70/30 her. I eventually conceded.

Martin Luther once called diaper changing a holy work. Why? Because it is an act of care that needs to be done. His point was that callings, even the most mundane, are of great significance. Our vocations don't necessarily bring happiness. But they do bestow significance. "I'm doing something that really matters."

In our newsfeeds and highlight reels, we look for the spectacular. Someone who gave her kidney away. Or took a bullet for someone else. Or started a new company from scratch. By comparison, we feel inadequate and unaccomplished.

But what if the most spectacular feats were unsung and unnoticed? A diaper changed. A hug given. A meal made. A hopeful word. An hour of listening. A ride to work. What else could love look like? Where else would we see it so clearly?

This is important because God-inspired significance helps us to persist under pressure. When our callings are burdensome, the power of a call compels us to redouble our efforts. Proudly embrace the simple and sometimes dirty tasks that God places before you. Don't be ashamed of the mundane things you do day after day. **The love we show, the patience we muster, the attention we give—this is Christ living in and through us.**

HOW TO DISCOVER YOUR CALLING

These characteristics sound good, but how do you know where you are sent? How do I discover my calling? Some callings are naturally obvious. They seem to seek us out. Others are more subtle, and we must make decisive choices through heart-wrenching deliberation. Here are some principles to guide the discernment of our callings.

BEGIN WHERE YOU ARE

Before you get too far, don't miss the obvious. We frequently neglect the call of people and tasks that are right in front of our noses. Take a look around. Where are you? Who and what is around you? What are you already doing? Who currently depends on you? It could be that your calling is self-evident, right before your eyes. Or maybe your current circumstance will point you to an entirely new calling.

KNOW YOURSELF

The skinny 5'4" kid probably doesn't have the capacity to play professional basketball. That's okay. So what does he possess?

A prerequisite to discerning a calling is self-awareness. What are my strengths, gifts, interests, and abilities? What are my liabilities and weaknesses? Where are my gaps? What experiences make me uniquely qualified?

To be truly self-aware, it is necessary to seek help. Share your deliberation with others. Seek trusted counsel and be ready to listen and receive their words. Confront sentimental or unrealistic dreams. Ask someone what he or she sees in you. God works through people in your life. We need their advice, insight, and encouragement. They will both challenge and affirm you.

KNOW YOUR WORLD

If our vocations are for other people, then we must be aware of our neighbors' context. What are the needs around me? What suffering exists?

What needs to get done? What do I possess that might help? What role do I have in the broader scheme of things?

This assumes that we live in and love the community around us. It means we must be reasonably familiar with society's issues. We listen to our neighbors. We walk the streets and roads. We shop the stores.

KNOW WHERE YOU'RE INDISPENSABLE

No one is completely indispensable. God can do his work without us. Yet he chooses to use us to accomplish specific and necessary work. In determining a particular calling, it's important to know where you're uniquely positioned to make a difference.

When you know yourself and your world, you begin to identify urgent needs. Ask, "What is it that if I don't do it, no one can or will?" You have a skill to bring, a voice to speak, or a perspective to impart. There are some things that another could do just as well as I can. But there are other things that only I can do, or can do extraordinarily well.

PRAY

It may seem obvious, but don't miss the priority of prayer. At the end of all your great thinking, you might still be confused. Or after all your schemes and strategy, you may well be misguided. We need more than a well-thought plan. We need illumination from the Spirit of God.

Prayer keeps us from believing that our callings are about us. Those who are called by God must call on him. In calling upon God, we acknowledge that all our callings come from him. We submit our skills, time, energy, and ability to him. We allow him to ultimately govern and guide our lives. "Thy will be done" is our concluding statement of faith.

As we pray, we often find serendipitous opportunities that arise. An unexpected offer comes. A brand-new friendship is formed. A new skill is discovered. What seems to be "out of the blue" is actually divinely arranged and provided for.

TRUST

At the end of all these things, are you still confounded? Occasionally we find ourselves paralyzed by a decision. "What if I make the wrong choice?" When we are at an end, we find ourselves in the perfect place for faith. At some point, *just choose.* Make a decision. Go. Take action.

You have callings that are filled with uncertainty. You might shiver with fear to take the first step. When God calls you to something, it's not neatly packaged or clearly mapped out. So you just start walking. And you trust that when you take a step, there is ground underneath. That is faith.

Many of our decisions are between two good things for which there is no "wrong answer." Just step forward and trust that God will go before you on the road. Our callings are not a complicated maze of options for which only one road is our destiny. There is freedom in our vocations. There is grace in determining our callings.

PRIORITIES

How do you live out your callings? How do you do them well? A multitude of temptations detract. We multitask and never get anything done. We are overcommitted. We are distracted. We say "yes" to everything. In a fast-paced society, we're too busy to effectively stay focused on a few key things. The result is stress, burnout, and poor health.

Our vocations give us clear priorities. They keep us focused on where we're sent. Here are some practical ways that vocation can keep us focused on what matters most, and defend against unhealthy busyness:

WHAT ARE THE TOP FIVE PRIORITIES IN YOUR LIFE?

List your top five. Post them on your mirror, your refrigerator, or anywhere you will see them every day. These should be the ultimate things God calls you to, such as: faith in him, a spouse, children, friends, career, etc.

DOES YOUR SCHEDULE REFLECT YOUR PRIORITIES?

Look at your last month. Just by looking at your calendar, could someone identify your top five priorities? Where did you spend most of your time? Are you busy with the wrong things?

SCHEDULE EVERYTHING

You have a work or school schedule. You schedule doctor and dentist appointments. Do you schedule family time? Do you schedule time for rest or exercise? Do you schedule time for worship and prayer? Often the items at the top of our priority list don't make the calendar. We assume that we'll get to them, but if they don't make the calendar, we don't follow through.

CREATE BOUNDARIES

What lines are hard? What lines cannot be crossed? Draw those lines right now. Boundaries protect priorities and give you focus. For instance, on a day off, commit to not checking email. Or set aside a dinner hour when the TV is off and phones are set aside.

MANAGE NOTIFICATIONS

One of the great challenges to priorities today is our ability to be contacted anywhere at any time. Email, social media, calls, and texts. Our phones have the ability to push lower priorities up higher. Notifications can make unimportant things urgent. Limit your notifications to high priorities. Only check email or Facebook at designated times, not 20 times throughout the day.

LET SOME THINGS GO.

If you seriously evaluate your God-given callings, you'll recognize that you have to let some things go. You have to say "no" to lower priorities. You may have to decline some commitments, not do the softball league, or pass on the additional overtime shift.

Time and energy are finite resources. You are limited. You can't do everything . . . *and that's okay.* God is "on" all the time. He takes care of you even when you don't complete all the tasks you wanted to do. God is gracious enough to give you a few really important callings. Do those things really well.

• • •

I took a blank piece of paper and asked Brandon, "What are your challenges?" He thought for a moment and listed a series of difficulties. Money. His stutter. Transportation. Someone who accused him of stealing a wallet at the community college. I filled up the edges of the page.

"Now, answer this. Where do you see yourself in five years? I'm not just talking about a job or making money. I'm talking about what you're really called to do."

Without hesitation, he spit words out. I scribbled them down on the center of the sheet. "Helping kids." "Go back to my neighborhood." "My own business." "Programs for children." "Mentoring." "Tutoring." "Training." He ended with, "I want to change a life. Like mine's been changed."

The white page was no longer blank. I circled two key items that represented a theme. "Kids." "Change a life." This was a calling, a transcendent claim upon his life. It superseded all the other words on the page. It was who God made Brandon to be, and the needs God placed in front of him.

Brandon took the page off the table and tucked it in his backpack. I said, "I'm proud of you." He smiled for the first time that afternoon and picked up his spoon to eat his soup.

Reflect

> Set aside some time to map out your specific imprint of vocations. Compile a list of your specific callings under each of the four spheres: Home, Occupation, Society, Congregation.

> Three characteristics of calling were listed. Callings are God-given, for the sake of others, and they give significance. Which of these rings especially true for you?

> In making an important decision about a calling, have you experienced any of the principles listed under "How to Discover Your Calling"?

> How do vocations give us a sense of purpose and meaning? How does this carry you through on days when you feel like giving up?

GO

It was fairly embarrassing, a grown man twitching and bouncing to Nineties pop music. We were having a raucous family dance party. The kids were spinning and jumping. My wife busting a move, quite well I might add. And then there was me, the dad awkwardly attempting to keep a beat.

Something in the window caught my eye. Two eyes and a nose pressed against the glass. Someone was standing in our front shrubbery, peering into our home. It turned out to be three faces of the wandering neighbor girls from down the street.

These three girls regularly strolled down the sidewalk and poked into our yard for something to do. They found friendship among our children, my daughter Emily in particular. With a heart of hospitality, Emily welcomed them in for snacks. She set tea parties for them and shared her dolls. I tended to be annoyed by their intrusions, but Bobbi said, "They're just little girls looking for a home."

Our house is a large brick structure that's more than 100 years old. It used to be a two-family flat. It's a bigger house than we ever thought we'd own. When we purchased it, we vowed to use it for God and for neighbors. My wife reminds me of that pledge when my introverted self wants a quiet house.

Our house represents all that "loved" means. I can open the front door after a tragic day and smell the hamburger browning for lasagna. I join the rowdy laughter around the dining room table. We plunge into the post-dinner ritual of wrestling in the living room. A dance party ensues. We tuck the kids in after prayers, songs, and stories. Thanks in large part to my wife, our home is safe, inviting, and open.

But we cannot remain behind the safety of these fortress walls. Every morning we leave the refuge of home and dispatch to our various places of work. One particular morning my nine-year-old daughter was hesitant.

"Bella, you okay?" I asked.

"Yeah." Her response was unconvincing.

"Is Brandon bothering you again?" Brandon was a fellow fourth-grader in her class.

"Yeah." Now she was telling the truth.

"What's up?"

"He follows me. And he called me a 'B.'"

"Did you tell a teacher?"

"Yeah, but he just finds a way to keep doing it."

When selecting a school years earlier, there were safer options, schools in better neighborhoods with great test scores. We could have sent her to a private school, a school with a more established and stable environment. Instead we chose an urban charter school that was just launching.

As white kids, our children are minorities in classrooms of varying color. Middle class, they study next to kids of diverse socioeconomic backgrounds. Our children come from a two-parent home. A majority of their peers are raised by a single parent or grandma.

Our school choice was deliberate. We celebrated the diversity, but Brandon's bullying challenged my conviction. *Maybe we should have made a safer choice.* The paternal impulse is powerful, especially for daughters.

What was this kid doing to my little girl? I imagined myself interrogating Brandon like a detective, him sitting in a cold steel chair under a bright, hot light bulb. Then I reminded myself, "Come on, Jeff, he's only a fourth-grade boy."

That weekend, I picked up "my Brandon" for dinner. As we drove, I lamented the antics of fourth-grade Brandon.

"I thought all Brandons were nice guys."

He chuckled.

"No, seriously, what should I do? This kid won't leave her alone."

"Bring me with you. I'll tell 'em what's up."

"He's in fourth grade."

"Oh . . . no matter."

"I've given him the eye a couple times when I went to pick Bella up."

"The eye?"

"You know, intimidating. Like this." I glared at him till the light turned green. He giggled again.

"What's he doin'?"

"He pushes her. And he called her a 'B.'"

"I done that before. Not that I'm proud of it. Said it to a girl back in the third grade."

"Brandon, you're not helping me, man."

It was then that the obvious hit me. Fourth-grade Brandon had a story, just like "my Brandon" did. Everyone comes from somewhere. I knew that fourth-grade Brandon had no father. His mother recently got out of jail. He had learning disabilities. His behavior showed characteristics of fetal alcohol syndrome.

Cursing my daughter is not excusable. But there was more behind it. Fourth-grade Brandon's story was similar to that of "my Brandon." By God's grace, big Brandon was given a way out. The right people were sent into his life. Who was sent to fourth-grade Brandon? Who would show him love? Bella?

I shivered at the thought that just infiltrated my mind. I live and preach the words "loved" and "sent." But now they were too real. It wasn't just a catchy tagline. This was life and family.

From the passenger seat next to me, Brandon recounted his grade school foolishness. "Aww, she be okay," he concluded. "She knows who she is."

The world is not safe. I suppose we could build quiet monasteries to escape. Or I could lock my family behind the fortress walls of our house. Or move to a remote compound in the Mountain West. But there is no utopia in any city, suburb, or rural town. No person or place is immune to tragedy, pain, and strife.

Every morning, I drop my kids off at school. I recite a statement for each one of them as they prepare to stumble out the door. For Bella and Emily I say, "You're my special girl. I love you very much. Have a great day." If I forget to say it, they glare at me, as if I've forgotten a necessary component of their day.

Bella is loved, by God and by me. From that love she is sent, even and especially to people suffering an absence of love. Even and especially to "fourth-grade Brandons." Still, it's hard to trust that God's hands are strong enough to hold her when I'm not around. I struggle to believe that God can use her to impact the life of someone like Brandon.

It's not easy, but I cannot escape the burden of the word upon my heart. In the face of the hardest challenges, the word "sent" says, "go."

. . .

Ava's view of Christianity is shared by many. To varying degrees, non-Christians believe that Christians want to force their beliefs on everyone. "Christians just preach at you." "They shove the Bible down your throat." "I got the 'Jesus lecture.'" "They tell me what to believe, but they don't even know me."

The term "evangelism" has conjured images of men in suits pounding on your door and asking if you're "saved." You cringe as you peer around the corner. Before you can say, "hello," they literally attempt to scare the hell out of you. "If you were to die tonight, do you know where you would go?" You think, "Well, hell sounds really bad. So I guess . . . heaven?"

Christians aren't the only ones capable of an imposing demeanor. Politics, business, and entertainment all intrude upon us with their message. They strong-arm a forceful conversion to their product or point of view. When approached in this fashion, the Christian mission can be perceived as:

MANIPULATIVE

I selfishly bend other people to my will and way of life. The goal is to get them to be like me. Life is easy when everyone agrees with me. This kind of evangelism fears those who are different.

COLONIAL

Here, evangelism is less about Jesus and more about culture. The goal is to advance Christian culture (whatever that may be) and not Christ himself. With arrogance or like a bully, the church is an empire imposing its language and customs.

FEAR-BASED

Too often the Christian feels an unbearable burden of responsibility for the eternal destiny of others. With the focus more on the Christian than Christ, I shoulder what only God is responsible for. It's often called a "messiah complex." I believe that I must save people, when in fact only Jesus does this. So I take credit when someone comes to faith. And I despair when I can't get someone to believe.

Twisted versions of evangelism exist. But this does not diminish the necessity of bearing witness to our faith. Someone once told me, "If you don't share what you believe, no one will ever know who you are." We are most authentic when we reveal our deeply held convictions. This is not done out of manipulation or fear. *Christian witness is simply expressing who we are.*

SENT

While the Great Commandment hinges on the word "love," Jesus' Great Commission centers on the word "go." "Therefore go and make disciples of all nations, baptizing them in the name of the Father and of the Son and of the Holy Spirit, and teaching them to obey everything I have commanded you" (Matt. 28:19–20). "Go" is the command of the one who sends. It recalibrates any misaligned approach to Christian mission.

I mentioned at the outset that the word "mission" comes from the Latin *missio,* which means "to send." The Biblical words for "sent" (both in Hebrew and Greek) carry a deep and indelible relationship with the "one who sends." "Sent" not only links the sender and the recipient, but also unites the sender with the one who is sent.

In other words, "sent" is not just a mechanical transmission. This would be like postal workers. They simply deliver letters or packages. There is no substantive connection between the mail carrier and the sender. They don't know who sent you junk mail. They don't know Aunt Betty who sent you a Christmas card (with ungodly amounts of silver glitter). They are just the messengers.

By contrast, a Biblical use of "sent" implies that a piece of "the sender" goes with the one who is "sent." More than an impersonal delivery, "sent" requires personal contact. It's like an ambassador sent to represent the sender *in person.* The ambassador's handshake, words, and message would be as if the sender were there. **The sender and the one sent are tied to one another.**

God sends agents, not merely as transmitters, but as those who bear in their person his own love. Like ambassadors, agents, or emissaries, the "sent ones" extend the authority and power of the sender. Jesus' mission continues in every era. His words prove true millennia later: "And surely I am with you always, to the very end of the age" (Matt. 28:20).

I was once talking to a Liberian pastor. We were discussing water wells in his West African country. He said that sending money and resources from America was important, but that it often missed something more vital. He said, "That's fine, but your presence means more than what you can bring." The love of God is bound up in people. This is why the primary movement of his mission is the deployment of persons, not objects, supplies, or religious literature.

It's also critical to understand that the focus of the word "sent" is more on its **originator** than its object. The Hebrew word for "sending" has this sense in Isaiah 6:8: "Then I heard the voice of the Lord saying, 'Whom shall I send? And who will go for us?' And I said, 'Here am I. Send me!'" The focus is **the sender's goal, will, intention, and desired outcome.** Only secondarily is it about the one who is sent. Thus we use the word "sent" in passive form.

Christian mission that is overly obsessed with the "sent ones" will invariably become manipulative, colonial, and fear-based. These attempts come across as abusive, insensitive, and desperate. It's more about the self than the one who sends.

When the focus is on the sender, the "sent ones" find a compelling charge with which to embark. Mission becomes natural and freeing. I find that I am a critical part of God's mission in the world, even as I am replaceable. God could do without me, yet he chooses to employ my best (and sometimes worst) efforts for his purpose. As Charles Haddon Spurgeon once noted, "We work as if it all depended on us, and we know that it all depends on God."

To "go" is a scary thing. We are fraught with fear and a sense of inadequacy. In the New Testament, there are a couple words for "sent." A particularly powerful term is *apestello*. From it we get the word "apostle," which means, "sent one." This word means, **"to be sent with the authority of the sender."** There is a power behind the sending because the sender has given it. This supplies courage to trembling agents of Christ. The sender imparts *his* authority.

Jesus expressed this divine authorization when he said, "As the Father has sent me, even so I am sending you" (John 20:21). The perfect Sent One is Jesus, deployed by the Father on a worldwide rescue mission. The startling part of this sentence is "even so." Just as Jesus was sent, "even so" his followers. With divine assistance from the Holy Spirit (John 15:26–27), Christians are sent to testify to God's love revealed in the sending of Christ (John 3:16).

This focus on the sender illustrates that all mission is **God's mission,** often referred to as the *Missio Dei.* He is the beginning and end of all sending. Human strategy, planning, and inspiration are secondary to the sender's initiative. "Sent ones" are those who "get in on" what God has already been doing as he reconciles the whole world to himself. We surrender ourselves to his inspiration.

PLAN A

I am convinced that every follower of Jesus is sent to at least one person. There is no Christian who is *not* sent. We are to embody the love of God in Christ to one person (at least) who is in need of this love. My good friend Robert Millar puts it this way: "You are God's Plan A for someone, and there is no Plan B." I suppose God could have a plan B or C. But the point is that Jesus' commission comes to us with serious intention.

At least in Western Christianity, much of the church has come to rely on professionals to do the mission. There is an idea that it takes a pastor or trained missionary to rightly and accurately speak the Gospel. If the growth of God's church were dependent only on the professional, Christianity would be a minor religious sect in a small pocket of the globe. Instead, it's a worldwide movement.

Compared to the professional, most Christians feel unqualified. This is evidenced by a deference to the seminary-trained pastor or a charismatic leader. Unlike the one behind the pulpit, we feel like a liability to God's mission.

Nonetheless, Scripture is filled with weak, lowly, quiet, and ordinary missionaries. Jesus' 12 disciples were not seminary-trained or even college-educated. They were skilled in their various trades. Training in the kingdom of God came from three years of living with Jesus. It seems to me that being with Jesus is a good qualification for being sent.

I don't want to undermine the importance of ongoing training or equipping. Nor do I suggest that every Christian has the same gifting in regard to the mission. Not everyone is called to publicly preach or skillfully debate. Still, every Christian is sent, for someone, for something.

Those who are loved by God are sent by him, precisely because they are loved. Most Christians are subversive missionaries. They go to schools, stores, and places of work with the Gospel subtly imbedded in their being. They fulfill the Great Commission in the course of their ordinary daily lives. And thus the kingdom of God steadily advances through his people. Every person plays his or her unique role, and in various ways they carry out their orders as "sent ones."

RELATIONAL WITNESS

The Gospel naturally runs along relational lines. In this way, Christian witness is simpler than a scripted speech or the awkward distribution of Christian literature on a street corner. Though an evangelist preaching to thousands has a role, exponential transmission of God's love in Christ occurs through the multitude of God's people living in relationships. It is critical to express our faith in real, natural, everyday relationships with those around us. Here are some key ways we do that:

BUILD RELATIONSHIPS

You have an extensive network of relationships—family, friends, coworkers, and neighbors. No one has your exact matrix of connections. See this network as the first place that God has sent you. *Invest in these relationships.* If you don't know a non-Christian person, then join your neighborhood association or volunteer with a non-Christian nonprofit. Join your local fitness club, coach Little League, or join a book club.

EARN THE RIGHT TO BE HEARD

This is a line from the mission organization Young Life. Don't talk until you've earned the right. Don't talk until you've done a lot of listening. Don't speak until you've been asked. If you speak too quickly, you'll fall right into the stereotype of every pushy, judgmental, arrogant Christian they've ever met. But once they trust you, your words will carry power.

BE OKAY WITH QUESTIONS

I feel the need to have a neat, tidy answer for every question. But the quick, canned statement that we recite off the laminated cheat sheet comes across as demeaning and condescending. No one likes the kid who thinks he or she knows it all.

Instead of preaching the answer, wrestle through it *with* them. You don't need to be defensive. God can defend himself. Taking someone's question seriously means that you take the person seriously. Honoring their struggle honors them. God is big enough to engage those who wrestle with him.

TELL YOUR STORY

With regularity Israel recounted what God had done for them (Ex. 15:1–18; Deut. 6:20–23). Early Christians were always retelling the story of what God was doing in Jesus (Acts 2:22–24; I Cor. 15:1–11). In short, God's people are storytellers.

In business, the best advertisement is personal customer satisfaction. Referrals are powerful. You trust your friends and their experience. In sharing your faith with a non-Christian person, you don't have to spew statements or recite talking points. There will be a time for further explanation. But first, **tell your own story.** They really want to know. What compels *you* about this Christ? Why do *you* follow Jesus? What has God done for *you?* *If you don't have a good reason, they won't either.*

T. S. Eliot once wrote, "The greatest proof of Christianity for others is not how far a man can logically analyze his reasons for believing, but how far in practice he will stake his life on his belief." Be honest about who you are. Be clear about what you're willing to stake your life on.

Could you tell three stories about God's work in your life? Could you answer why you follow the Man from Nazareth? Could you comment on your experience of God's grace? Could you recount a time you saw God's power? You might refer to the worst day of your life, or the greatest blessing you've been given, or the hardest thing you've ever done. There is a story in these moments of our lives. Our friends are waiting to hear our deepest convictions in these stories.

TELL *THE* STORY

Your story is great, but it leads to a greater story. It is the preface to the transcendent narrative that will apply to your friend. So tell that story. Be able to answer basic questions like, "What's the Bible all about?" "Who is Jesus? Why is he important?" "What do you believe about God?"

For me, "loved" and "sent" are simple words that are Biblical while at the same time common in our everyday language. In other words, by themselves they don't carry the baggage of religious jargon. This is a neutral starting point.

From here I can say things like:

"I believe in a God who loves the unlovable."

"I'm convinced of a love that proved itself in blood."

"The Bible is all about a messy people and a God of love who sends them help no matter how deep they've sunk."

"I believe we're loved more than we can imagine and sent with more purpose than we thought."

With this short bridge, I can expand to broader themes in the story. Creation, redemption, and sanctification. God creates, wins back, and transforms. Or you could expound on the simple handles of the Gospel in the manger, cross, and crown. Tell the story of Jesus' life, death, and resurrection. Apply them to others' personal circumstances. Do they need the presence of God? Are they desperate for pardon or forgiveness? Are they weak and in need of Christ's word of power?

The bottom line in speaking the Gospel is that we ourselves know it intimately. Those who have walked the land describe it best. Those who are themselves loved will naturally illustrate that love for others.

PRAY

No, seriously. Pray. People's lives are messy. Hearts are hard. There are people about whom we might say, "They are impossible. They will never, ever be open to God." But impossibility is the perfect place for prayer. Jesus said, "If you have faith as small as a mustard seed, you can say to this mountain, 'Move from here to there,' and it will move. Nothing will be impossible for you" (Matt. 17:20).

Prayer is an act of faith. By praying we say, "Only God can do this." You can't save a person. Only God does that. So return to the core belief that this is the sender's mission, not yours.

KNOW THAT GOD USES WEAK THINGS

You might feel weak, foolish, or like a failure. You might feel absolutely inadequate to talk about what you believe with others. *Will they judge me? Will they question my core convictions? What if they ask a question I don't know the answer to? What if I say the wrong thing?*

Remember that the cross looked like a failure. When Jesus died, it looked like God lost. Paul says, "God chose what is foolish to shame the wise. God chose what is weak to shame the strong. God chose what is low and despised, and the things that are not, to bring to nothing the things that are" (I Cor. 1:27–29). God has a track record of using failure to gain victory.

Contrary to the pretty and popular people we place on pedestals, God's greatest agents are not of the perfect pedigree. We claim that God especially uses people who are awkward, unexpected, and underwhelming. In fact, our weakness offers an even greater opportunity for God's power to emerge.

Jesus says, "Go," but we prefer safety to discomfort and stability to risk. If we keep the bar low, we can't fail. Yet the words of Jesus challenge our propensity for conservative and carefully calculated Christian living. The Father's "sending" took Jesus to resistance, dishonor, and suffering. Jesus said, ". . . even so I am sending you." So we expect the challenges we've seen our Master encounter.

It is dangerous to be sent. But the real danger is in *not going*. When Jesus tells us to go, it's dangerous to stay. Our courage in being sent arises from the fact that we don't go alone. We are sent with the presence, pardon, and power of Jesus himself. He goes with us always, "to the end of the age" (Matt. 28:20).

• • •

As a kindergartner, Bella had a Muslim classmate. One day she described a conversation she had: "Yeah, she wears a scarf on her head. She doesn't know about Jesus so I told her about the manger, cross, and crown." The culturally sensitive corner of my brain was horrified. But then I thought, "Isn't this how we've raised her?" She had a natural confidence that I lacked. Her identity is in Jesus, and she was simply being herself.

In first grade she came home and said that her best friend wanted to be baptized. "I told her about Jesus," she stated calmly. I was more concerned about what her parents would say. A few weeks later, Bella's best friend and her younger sister were baptized.

Now in fourth grade, Brandon was a tougher case. He was one of the "impossibles." He was beyond repair. His only destiny was "hell or jail." Just when I think that someone is beyond repair, I remember a mentor's words: "We love people in their lostness. After all, God does." No one is too far for God. There is no "beyond repair" from his vantage point.

Bobbi gave me some perspective: "I think Brandon likes Bella."

"Yeah? Why do you think that?"

"Well, she's one of the only people who's kind to him. She refuses to pick on him."

"Then why does he bully her?"

"He doesn't know how to show kindness back."

"Well, he better learn."

"I'm just saying that he's trying to get her attention. He's desperate for someone to care."

My wife was right. Toward the end of the school year a note was stuffed in Bella's backpack. The handwriting was barely legible. But it clearly stated, "Bella, sorry I been mean. I think your speshil. Brandon."

The following year, little Brandon didn't return to the school. So many of our city's children are subject to a transient life. They move from one apartment to another, staying with an aunt one day and grandma the next. It's not uncommon for a kid to switch schools every year. Without any stability, the child's identity and purpose are shaped by the cold streets they wander. I pray for fourth-grade Brandon, wherever he is.

Reflect

> What are common perceptions of the word "evangelism"? How does this affect society's perception of Christians?

> How does the word "sent" combat a Christian mission that is manipulative, colonial, or fear-based?

> How does a definition of the word "sent" empower us when we're overwhelmed by the seriousness of God's command to "go"?

> Take some time to identify three to five people you believe God is sending you to.

> Refer to the key practices under "Relational Witness." Among those you are sent to, which key practice is critical for you?

CONCLUSION

Ava and Jacob sit across from each other at the diner. An elderly couple sips coffee and shares a plate of pancakes. A professional-looking man in his fifties sits alone, eating whole-wheat toast and scanning his tablet.

Time is frozen. In this pocket of a moment, Ava realizes that this encounter is awkward. *Why did I ask him to have coffee? I bet he thought I was asking him out. Oh, God!* She can't undo the last hour. She said what she said. So she wonders, *What will he say?*

In the same moment, Jacob wonders why he's here with Ava. *But I'm here. So I guess I should say something.* He feels compassion for the girl under the thorny exterior. He hurts as he glances at the jagged scars on her wrists. *God, this girl needs your love. You've sent me here. Help me say something that's good for her.*

For Christians, these moments aren't random. They are divinely serendipitous. Those who are loved by God are sent by him. There is no person loved by God who is *not* sent. Like Jacob to Ava, or in less dramatic ways, we are all deployed to a variety of people desperate for God's love.

The prospect of God sending you to an Ava is harrowing. But you don't have to look far. There are "Avas" in your family, down the street, at work, and at school. The Great Commandment and the Great Commission place us under divine orders: "Love." "Go." You cannot escape the people right in front of you.

As much as **loved** and **sent** provide me with identity and purpose, they also devastate me with their great demand. If the "loved" are sent to love the same way God does, I seriously question my ability. I don't naturally love like God. The personal cost is too high. "I can't do that," I retort. "It's impossible."

What lures me back is that these words are passive. It's not that *I* love the world, but "*God* so loved the world . . ." We don't initiate the loving or sending. The passive form of these words means *we just are*. Only because we *are* loved are we able *to* love. Only because we are *sent* are we able to *go*. God gives the necessary ability to match the occasion. He speaks to my trembling heart: **"You are loved more than you can imagine and sent with more purpose than you thought."**

Jesus' ministry was not only defined by words, but also by actions. There was a certain way in which he dealt with people. Grace and truth emanated from his earthly life. His Gospel was not a sterile doctrine, an esoteric idea. It was a personal reality of sacrificial love. His was, and is, a love that gives itself and bears our burden.

"Loved" and "sent" are not meant to be endlessly lectured. They are not words in a textbook. They have *been* done, and they are meant to *be* done. They are God's activity *done to us*. Then they become God's directive, *done through us*.

God's love must continually be embodied in the love that seeks lost people. The credibility of the church's message depends on whether the church will go in response to God's sending. Our relational capital is only earned when we make the burden of others our own. Therefore "loved" and "sent" are not divergent activities. In tandem, they are one expression of God's heart.

I have a habit of imagining the future. Bobbi says I'm crazy. But seeing the future gives me perspective. The Psalmist expresses this: "So that the next generation would know, even the children yet to be born, and they in turn would tell their children" (Ps. 78:6). I often think about my children's children. I pray that they might know the great and mighty deeds of God.

As I write this, my children are relatively young. The baby of our family is two years old. His name is Jacob. I picture him someday in the future. I imagine him as the young man sitting across the table from Ava in the diner. Ava may be a toddler today. Maybe she isn't even born. But one day Jacob will meet her. In fact, he will be sent to many "Avas" in his lifetime.

What will Jacob say? How will he answer the question, "Who are you?" I ponder in the present what my children will say and do in the future. They must have a clear, concise, consistent, and compelling answer.

I hold Jacob at bedtime in his room decorated with dinosaurs. We read his favorite book, *Goodnight, Moon*. We pray. I hold him. His head is nestled at the point where my shoulder meets my neck. His breathing falls into its nocturnal rhythm. I sing the old hymn, "Abide with Me."

Before I lay the boy down into his bed, I imagine Jacob as a man, years from now. He's sitting at that table in the diner. After telling her story, Ava asks, "Well, who are you?" Jacob takes a deep breath and begins, "Let me tell you my story. I am loved by God, and I believe he sent me to you . . ."

QUANTITY DISCOUNTS

You can purchase additional copies for your team or study group at significant savings by ordering direct. The retail price of *Loved and Sent* is $15.99. You can save up to 40%.

Quantity	Price per copy	Shipping	Total
4	$12	$7	$55
20	$11	$13	$233
40	$10	$17	$417
80	$9	Free	$720

Simply email your order to jeff.cloeter@gmail.com.